You've Got • The
Interview
NOW WHAT?

You've Got • the
Interview
NOW WHAT?

Fortune 500 Hiring Professionals
Tell You How to Get Hired

Brenda Greene

Dearborn™
Trade Publishing
A **Kaplan Professional** Company

President, Dearborn Publishing: Roy Lipner
Vice President and Publisher: Cynthia A. Zigmund
Senior Acquisitions Editor: Michael Cunningham
Development Editor: Karen Murphy
Senior Project Editor: Trey Thoelcke
Interior Design: Lucy Jenkins
Cover Design: Depinto Design
Typesetting: Elizabeth Pitts

Published by Dearborn Trade Publishing
A Kaplan Professional Company

Printed in the United States of America

05 06 07 10 9 8 7 6 5 4 3 2 1

Library of Congress Cataloging-in-Publication Data

Greene, Brenda.
    You've got the interview—now what? : fortune 500 hiring professionals tell you how to get hired / Brenda Greene.
        p.   cm.
    Includes bibliographical references and index.
    ISBN-13: 978-1-4195-1132-5
    1. Employment interviewing—Handbooks, manuals, etc. 2. Job hunting—Handbooks, manuals, etc.   I. Title.
    HF5549.5.I6G76   2005
    650.14′4—dc22

                                                            2005013980

To my mother and father,
Who always worked hard . . . for others

The job applicant's gray suit is neatly pressed, his tie is just the right shade of red, and he just caught a peek of his clean-shaven face in the office window. His hair, which has just been trimmed, is behaving itself for once. He is sitting up straight, looking squarely at the HR manager, and smiling. He's feeling pretty good about himself as he sits at a table in the human resources department of Big, Inc.

And why shouldn't he! He just spent the last three days getting to know everything there is to know about this leviathan of a company. He knows the names; he has the numbers. He is all pumped up and can't wait to casually throw in that Big, Inc., had a 20.8 percent sales growth in 2005. And just in case the HR manager is more intuitive than traditional, he hasn't neglected his mindset either. In fact, he spent the better part of the preceding day murmuring positive self-talk and rehearsing "What if" scenarios that test his problem-solving skills. He even made sure he got a good night's sleep. He is thoroughly prepared for the interview.

That's when the HR manager looks directly at the job applicant, smiles back, and says, "How are you? Good. Let's get started. Tell me about a recent project that failed." Just like that Mr. Slam Dunk Interview Man is at a loss for words. His face turns red, he starts to mumble. Finally, he gathers his composure and pulls something out of his crumpled brain. He mentions the probability spreadsheet his boss threw on his desk accompanied by a copy of the book *Changing Careers for Dummies.* The job applicant smiles at the thought, but the HR manager fails to see the humor. An awkward silence is broken when the HR manager asks, "How can the new company help you develop?" The applicant recovers slowly by announcing his desire to pursue an MBA. He said he was hoping he could tap into the company's tuition reimbursement plan to cement that dream. Before the applicant can even ask his first question, the interviewer thanks him for his time, and the job applicant walks out of the office and wonders, "What was that all about?"

In a lackluster job market, many job applicants have asked themselves the same question. A job interview gone awry is disconcerting, but it's not all that unusual in this hiring landscape. Nowadays companies can afford to be choosy. A front page headline in the St. Paul *Pioneer Press* read: "56 Cellists, 1 Position."[1] The job market is competitive—and not just for cellists. Every profession has been hard-hit by a downsized economy. In fact, most HR decision makers spend the bulk of their time disqualifying applicants rather than hiring them.

Even if applicants have spent weeks or months priming their résumés and cover letters for targeted jobs and made hard-won inroads at companies, they still have to ace the interviews—whether it's the first, second, or third time they have met with someone at the prospective company. For many, the final stage of the job search is the most daunting, simply because each job interview differs from the last one and the desired result—an offer—depends on so many variables.

So how do job seekers prepare for an interview? One way is by knowing what the expectations are at America's largest corporations. In *You've Got the Interview,* Fortune 500 hiring managers were asked what separates the garden-variety candidate from the job applicant who gets the offer. The results were surprising.

You have probably heard about "the right fit," but do you know exactly what that means? The Fortune 500 hiring professionals surveyed for this book give you an in-depth understanding of what constitutes "fit," but here is the first clue: it goes way beyond skills and qualifications. In fact, it has more to do with who you are as a person—the inner substance that drives you—than the degree you have from a prestigious university. Think integrity, accountability, energy, and initiative; and you will be closer to the crux of "fit."

Based on the input of Fortune 500 hiring professionals, this book helps you look at your work self in a new light—to discover how you can fit into that desirable position and get hired. Most of you already have the inner stuff that will make you successful in your working life. But to ace the interview in today's hiring territory, you have to know how to articulate the inner stuff. One of my aims is to provide you with the language you need to answer those delving questions. Another aim is to give you an inside look at how America's corporate giants arrive at their hiring decisions. The expectations are all laid out. It's up to you to decide whether you will meet them.

Finally, *You've Got the Interview* spurs you to think about your work self so that you can make a good match with a company, a company that provides you with satisfaction, fulfillment, and reward. It may sound like a tall order, but it's certainly attainable, especially if you treat a job search like a fact-finding mission. The Fortune 500 hiring professionals said it best: the more you know, the better the results. Follow their suggestions and you may find that perfect job—a job that taps into your talent, strengths, skills, and qualifications. You just have to know how to get it. The offer is waiting for those who do.

I am an optimist—or maybe my memory is just not so good. Either way, every time I undertake a book that bases its expertise on the input from professionals at the Fortune 500, I assume it is going to be a little easier to get the necessary information. I tend to forget that business—and life—are in a constant state of flux. Corporations change, people working there change, and everyone gets busier and busier.

I am always deeply grateful then that within this changing landscape executives at these massive corporations step up to offer their expertise. I applaud their generosity and knowledge. Completing this extensive survey takes time—probably the most valuable commodity of the 21st century—and considerable thought.

You've Got the Interview is my third book that has relied on the input of Fortune 500 professionals. As I did in *Get the Interview Every Time,* I surveyed Fortune 500 HR professionals to get an inside look on how job applicants get hired at these companies. The information they provided was revealing. To use a phrase from the tech world, these individuals are subject matter experts on the art of hiring.

But before I acknowledge their individual contributions, I would like to mention that participants are from companies on the 2004 Fortune 500 list.[1] Since the survey was conducted, some companies have merged or no longer rank in the Fortune 500. Some individuals, meanwhile, have moved to other companies or have been promoted. The list, for the most part, reflects the status of companies and individuals at the time I received responses to the survey. It should be mentioned also that the respondents' participation in the survey does not necessarily indicate an endorsement of this book.

With this said, I would like to extend my appreciation to the following human resources professionals for their time and thoughtful contribution:

- Allied Waste Industries, Inc.: Kathy O'Leary, Manager, Employment Services
- Alltel Corporation: Lara Crane, Manager of Staffing

- Baxter International, Inc.: Barbara Morris, Vice President of Human Resources
- BellSouth: Suzanne Snypp, Director, Human Resources/Staffing
- CarMax, Inc.: Pam Hill, Director of Staffing and Planning
- Continental Airlines: Mary Matatall, Director of Global Staffing
- Deere & Company: Sherri Martin, Director of Human Resources
- Energy East Management Corporation: Sheri Lamoureux, Director of Human Resources Planning
- Engelhard Corporation: Rocco Mangiarano, Director of Human Resources
- Fannie Mae: Trang Gulian, Manager of Human Resources
- Harley-Davidson Motor Company: Steve Duea, Manager of Staffing
- Health Net, Inc.: Diane Berk, Staffing Manager
- Host Marriott Corporation: Lisa Whittington, Senior Director of Human Resources
- HSBC North America Holdings Inc.: Brian K. Little, Group Director of Human Resources
- International Truck & Engine Corporation: Bill Vlcek, Manager of Strategic Staffing
- Jabil Circuit, Inc.: Heather Otto, Employment Manager
- Liz Claiborne, Inc.: Andrea Fenster, Director of Strategic Staffing
- Medco Health Solutions, Inc.: Audrey Goodman, Vice President of Organization Development
- Office Depot, Inc.: Anne Foote Collins, Director of Corporate Recruiting and Services
- Phelps Dodge Corporation: Art Calderon, Director of Human Resources and Strategic Programs
- PSEG Services Corporation: John Garofalo, Enterprise Staffing and Outreach Manager
- SYSCO Corporation: Amy Reeves, Director of Corporate Staffing
- TIAA-CREF: Robert Moll, Senior Human Resources Generalist
- Thrivent Financial for Lutherans: Debra Palmer, Staffing Manager
- The Timken Company: Barry Martin, Director of Staffing and Development

Beyond the surveys, many of the Fortune 500 HR professionals were available to answer questions throughout the writing of this book. In fact, I sought their feedback on many topics. I would like to set aside special thanks for their continued availability to Lisa Whittington, Barry Martin, Bill Vlcek, and Rocco Mangiarano.

In addition, I spoke with individuals at two other Fortune 500 companies. These conversations were thoroughly enjoyable and illuminating. The information they provided forms the basis of Chapter 6. Thank you to Neil Bussell, group manager, PepsiCo Business Solutions Group, whose input is based on his career experience, and Peter Thonis, senior vice president of external communications at Verizon.

I also received valuable direction and input from the following individuals: Helen Cunningham, director of communications at the Depository Trust & Clearing Corporation (DTCC); Dom Gallo, senior director of customer relationship management at Securities Industry Automation Corporation (SIAC); Anita Bruzzese, author and syndicated career columnist for Gannett; Kevin Marasco, marketing director at Recruitmax; Ted Horton, managing partner at BCI Partners; Jeanne Achille, president of the Devon Group; Chrystal McArthur, associate dean of Career Services at Rutgers University; Ruth Shlossman, a director at Watershed Associates; and Trina Lee, public relations manager at CarMax.

You've Got the Interview . . . Now What? is based on the information these professionals provided. Primarily, I followed their lead in the material I covered. There are, however, a few workplace lessons that I learned along the way. Those lessons have been woven in—a subtext of sorts—because I hope to save the reader the time it took me to understand that a successful career depends primarily on building good working relationships. I didn't quite get that when I was young and ambitious. Instead, I thought it was about working hard—period. I would have benefited from the career guidance these Fortune 500 professionals offer in this book.

I am also grateful to my editor, Jon Malysiak. It was originally his idea to write a follow-up book to *Get the Interview Every Time.* Jon then put me in the able hands of Karen Murphy and Trey Thoelcke, both excellent editors at Dearborn. This is the second book at Dearborn that Lois Sincere has copy edited for me and I would like to thank her for a thorough and thoughtful review of the text. My agent, Joelle Delbourgo, has been there from the very beginning, so I would like to extend my appreciation for her support, encouragement, and continued direction.

Finally, I would like to thank Myles, Rose Anna, and Marie Elena; Rose Greene; Mary Ellen and Nicky Caputo; Rosemary and Phil Chiavetta; Terrence and Mary Adele Byrne; Mary and Al D'Annibale; Doreen and Ray Murray; Patricia and Sylvester Leonard; Alice and Joel Good; Coleen and Megan Byrne; Donald Skinner; Sabina Horton; Sheila Nadata; Kathy Murphy; Sissy Cunningham; Martha Savant; and Suzann Anderson for their love and support.

1

WHAT THE FORTUNE
500 SURVEY SAYS

*"Be prepared to talk about your work in detail and
sound like you really want the job."*

AUDREY GOODMAN
Vice President of Organization Development
Medco Health Solutions, Inc.

To pry the doors open at a Fortune 500 company, you need top-notch skills and qualifications. You won't get an interview without them. But what you probably didn't realize is that your personal values play a key role in whether you will be hired. These values form the core that drives the offer. Without a doubt, those last two promotions listed on your résumé got you in the door, but it's your integrity, enthusiasm, accountability, and team orientation that often seal the deal. At least that was the major theme of a survey conducted in 2004–2005 of 25 Fortune 500 hiring professionals.

The respondents of the survey—Fortune 500 managers, directors, and vice presidents from human resources—said they want candidates who fit the job as well as fit the corporate culture. How they decipher *fit* depends on many factors; everything, in fact, from skills to personality. The 25 questions on the survey were formulated to reveal a more complete picture of the interview process at large corporations, but it was in the realm of personal values, attributes, and personality that the responses became particularly illuminating. In fact, a new set of capabilities seems to be emerging. So what exactly are the expectations of hiring managers?

You would be surprised by some of the answers. Of course, problem-solving, organizational, and communication skills rose to the top of the list of personal attributes but so did a strong work ethic, team orientation, respect for people, and accountability—qualities that are hard to evaluate within the normal one-hour time frame of an interview.

Perhaps that's one of the reasons why the trend to interview and then interview some more seems to be the norm. Today it's rare to jump on board after meeting only once with a prospective employer. Instead, multiple interviews with three, four, five people are commonplace—especially for senior-level positions. In fact, you may be scrutinized for hours before an offer is ever made. The interview process can be grueling—sweat inducing at times.

THE Q&A

The most incisive tools interviewers have at their disposal are the questions they ask candidates. The problem: "Describe your strengths and weaknesses" has morphed into such questions as "Describe what safety means to you as a personal value" or "What is your strongest criticism of yourself?" or "Describe your most challenging work environment and how you dealt with it" or "Describe a project that failed" or "What is your biggest regret?" These are the questions that can throw you off balance. After all, you came into the interview prepared to tell the employer how extraordinary you are. What's all this talk about difficulties and setbacks?

Brian Little, a group director at HSBC, said questions like the ones above "generally give the interviewee a chance to show introspection and also how he or she deals with adversity." Although most job interviews are conversational, behavior-based questions ("Give me an example when you . . .") are now standard forms of inquiry that are interwoven into the "conversation." Interviewers want to know what makes you tick, so they probe, and then they probe some more. You may be thinking that hiring professionals may be watching too much *CSI.* Actually, there's a good reason to evaluate prospective employees carefully. For one, replacing employees is costly.

Figures vary, but according to a recent article in the *New York Times,* "the cost of turnover per worker was $2,335,"[1] and according to another article in the same newspaper, an October 2004 study by the Employment Policy Foundation found that figure to be $13,355 "for a full-time private-sector worker."[2] Many Fortune 500 companies surveyed have 40,000 employees or more, so managing turnover is a priority. Add to that the fact that "about 22 percent of American workers voluntarily leave their jobs within the first year," and you can see a crisis brewing.

But an even more important reason hiring managers scrutinize prospective employees is that they know their companies are only as good as the people who work for them. That is where your personal values and attributes play into the equation. Employers value expertise, but a premium is also placed on candidates with good innards—those who are energetic, respectful, ambitious, hard working, positive, efficient, professional, credible, and trustworthy. Companies want employees who already exhibit these characteristics, because these qualities are next to impossible to develop in people who are resistant to them. In other words, you can go to all the management classes in the world and still act like a brute if you don't take the lessons to heart.

Add to this the fact that the hiring landscape is undergoing dramatic change technologically. It's not enough to know the meaning of the term *ASCII* (plain text). Now you need to familiarize yourself with computer software that, according to Kevin Marasco, a marketing director at Recruitmax, can actually help manage the "whole life cycle of the employee."

Still, it's the face-to-face interview that ultimately determines who makes the cut at most Fortune 500 companies. That's where HR professionals decide who fits and who doesn't. If you have made it to the interview stage, then that's a feather in the old *chapeau.* Congratulations. But now you want an offer, and to get it you need a good understanding of the new requirements. Otherwise, you may blow that one-hour opportunity that took you three months to create. To get an offer you have to know how to *answer* the questions, and you have to know how to *ask* the questions. And in the 21st century, the questions and answers have changed. But before going into the weighty substance of the interview, take a look at the following results of the Fortune 500 survey.

THE TIME IT TAKES

Generally, it takes one to three months for a Fortune 500 company to fill a position. In fact, only 20 percent[3] of the respondents said it "depends" on the position or it takes longer. PSEG is proud of its record in "averaging 40 days"; and Jabil Circuit makes a special notation that it has a "relatively quick turnaround" at 30 days, as does HSBC, but there are definitely no overnight successes. Filling positions is, in fact, a labor-intensive process, so a lot of care and planning go into the process. That's why these employers tend to be impatient with candidates who do no preparation for an interview. Many Fortune 500 respondents made a special point about how necessary it is for candidates to "do [their] homework."

Nearly unanimous, the Fortune 500 respondents agreed that a successful interview lasts about an hour. That does not mean, however, that you are in and out—with or without an offer—in that amount of time. That may be the time frame for the first interview. Then it's another hour for the next, and yet another hour for the one after that, and then.... Unless you are subjected to a panel interview, at some companies you can expect to meet up to seven or eight people before an employer offers you the job. But some Fortune 500 companies have turned the process into a science. Deb Palmer, a manager of staffing at Thrivent, said, "Our interview process is broken into multiple sections. The first on-site interview typically is 30 to 45 minutes with HR and 1 to 1.5 hours with a hiring manager or interview team."

So here's one of the first questions you can ask when you schedule an interview with a representative from human resources: "How does the process unfold at your company?" In other words, what's the routine? It differs significantly from one company to the next—and HR representatives are only too happy to answer this question because it saves them from being forced to cut you short at the first meeting during that 15-minute philosophical wax on your intricate understanding of Java.

When the respondents were asked how many interviews they conducted to fill a position, 28 percent said they conduct five or more, 8 percent said they conduct four interviews, 24 percent said they conduct three interviews, and 24 percent said they conduct two interviews; however, two company representatives said the two interviews are panel interviews, which means you may meet quite a few people before you're hired. Rocco Mangiarano, the director of human resources at Engelhard, said he normally conducts two interviews, but ten or more people may see the candidate before an offer is made. Nearly 16 percent of the respondents said it depends on the level of the position and, according to Bill Vlcek, manager of strategic staffing at International Truck & Engine, the higher the level, the more interviews.

Sometimes a candidate is escorted from one interview to the next the very same day. In fact, 52 percent of the respondents said this is normal procedure. But 36 percent said it depends on the position, because making the necessary arrangements on the spur of the moment is often impossible. Robert Moll, a senior human resources generalist at TIAA-CREF, said it "depends on the availability of hiring managers. Sometimes it is prearranged; occasionally, it happens spontaneously. Most often human resources first screens a few candidates for the hiring manager to see." Sheri Lamoureux, a director of human resources planning at Energy East, said following one interview with another is not typical: "We have variations as far as hiring practices. Some departments will have group hiring, where everyone interviews the candidate at the same time. What's more uncommon is that a candidate will go from one person to the next person. Hiring managers like to actually hear what the responses are to all of the questions together." There can be other variables as well. Anne Foote Collins, a director of recruiting and services at Office Depot, said the process "depends on the position and whether or not the applicant has had to travel for the interview." Only 12 percent of the companies said they do not follow one interview with the next—ever—on the same day.

Besides the level of the position, another element to be considered in the time frame is how eager the company is to scoop you up—or how dire the company's problem is that it needs to resolve. The important point is to make the job interview the primary objective of the day. If the first interview goes well, don't squelch the enthusiasm because you have another obligation that prevents you from meeting the next person in line. Stay focused on the interview because it is the most crucial stage of the whole arduous journey.

RED FLAGS AND GREEN LIGHTS

When asked to rate red flags—tardiness, unsuitable attire, lack of eye contact, poor communication skills—52 percent of the respondents said that *all* of these flags are equal and any one of them would set off alarm bells. But 28 percent of the respondents did rank poor communications skills as the number one alarm, whereas 4 percent said tardiness and the other 8 percent said unsuitable attire. Fortunately, there is no red flag that cannot be turned into a green light with a little effort.

These are the basics of a good first impression: be on time; wear neat and pressed business attire for job interviews; practice eye contact, and do some homework to ensure that your communication skills are up to speed during the Q&A. Don't knock yourself out of the running for a great job just because you made the assumption that the rules of the game apply to everyone else but you.

Two respondents added that the red flags given in the survey were not inclusive enough. Barry Martin, a director of staffing and development at Timken, said the most glaring red flag for him is "talking too much without listening." Engelhard's Mangiarano included, "all of the red flags mentioned; but what is particularly off putting to us is someone who doesn't answer the questions directly and tries to control the interview rather than letting the interviewer take control."

The survey addressed one red flag in more detail. In an era of casual dress, some candidates assume that they can show up at a job interview for a corporate position in less than their Sunday best. According to 8 percent of the respondents, this is a bad idea—even at a high-tech operation like Jabil Circuit, where some people would assume the environment is more casual. For the most part, men are expected to arrive in a suit and tie (or blazer and khaki pants) and women are expected to show up in business attire (either a dress suit or pants suit) for a job interview. John Garofalo, an enterprise staffing and resource manager at PSEG, said, "For professional and managerial positions, it is business attire. Bargaining-unit candidates are expected to wear the clothes they will wear on the job." But, again, do not neglect the basics: neat and pressed is the order of the day. Treat a job interview as a very big day in your life—because it is.

Some people assume that certain businesses or other areas—fashion, academic, entertainment—call for a more creative approach toward business attire. According to one Fortune 500 participant, "It's very important to ask, 'What is appropriate to wear for this interview?' That's not a question to be ashamed of asking. That's a question that shows... [the candidates] are thinking... [and] interacting. They want to do the right thing versus making an assumption."

Another requirement when you go to a job interview is that you bring several copies of your résumé. This was a unanimous response by the Fortune 500 hiring professionals. Every respondent said you should bring extra formatted résumés. You never know if you are going to spontaneously interview with another hiring manager during the course of an interview, so extra copies are essential. Not unanimous was whether candidates should bring a list of references. Only 36 percent thought a list adds a touch of professionalism. The remaining group said they have various other protocols when it comes to references. For instance, at PSEG, John Garofalo said, "We have introduced an e-reference report" (see Chapter 4 for more information), and Engelhard's Mangiarano said his searchers handle all reference checking ("I let them earn their money"). Play it safe, regardless. Bring a list of references. Many Fortune 500 companies request that candidates fill out an application form in addition to submitting a résumé, so you may need your reference information when you go for the face-to-face interview.

Although every career expert in America will tell you to write a thank you note after the interview, none of the respondents disqualify candidates because they haven't been personally thanked for their time. Still, the advice to express your gratitude is good. If you can craft a note that helps you to stand out above the competition, it will further your cause. But that also means that you may be writing six, seven, eight notes because everyone you meet with that day or the next should be acknowledged.

HOW'S YOUR TELEPHONE MANNER?

The first contact candidates have with a prospective employer is often through a telephone screen. Nearly 52 percent of the respondents said they always use the telephone screen to decide which applicants are suitable. That doesn't mean you won't get a call from the others: 28 percent of the respondents said they use a telephone screen "sometimes"; only two said they never use a telephone to screen out applicants. This means that job seekers must sell themselves as good candidates immediately and should be prepared to be quizzed in this initial conversation. What interviewers are primarily interested in hearing during the telephone screen is a brief overview of your qualifications and skills. The more delving questions are usually reserved for the face-to-face.

Here's what one Fortune 500 hiring professional said about the telephone screen: "We do telephone screening 80 percent of the time. When I first came here, there were a lot more face-to-face interviews. Since the growth in our company and general turnover in the industry, what I found is that it's very ineffective to just look at a résumé and invite someone in. You can't understand from that whether the person is going to be at the price point, whether the candidate has any flexibility in the price point, whether he or she can work in different locations. There are so many things that I think are important to establish. Does the person have an issue with the title change? We probably do a 20-minute telephone screen."

Discussing salary during the telephone screen is not unusual: 20 percent of Fortune 500 companies talk about your salary expectations. Usually, they are just trying to decide if you fall within their range—with specifics coming at the time an offer is made. But that means you have to have a rough estimate. That's why it's so important that you have an approximation of what you are worth in the marketplace. Maybe you sent a résumé to a big corporation more than a year ago and a position requiring your exact skills just opened. Always know what you are currently worth—in case an employer calls you unexpectedly.

DISCOVERING WHAT'S REQUIRED

Another area you may need to prepare for is a test or technical interview. Respondents said tests are usually administered in human resources in 40 percent of the companies surveyed; 16 percent said the tests were administered in the departments in which the candidate will work. Forty percent of the companies said they do not give any tests whatsoever to applicants (not including the technical interview for IT professionals), but one company reported the department gives the test; two companies reported that a third party administers it; and one company reported testing can take place in either HR or in the department. Actually, it is your responsibility to find out whether a test will be required for the position you are interviewing for. In some fields, it is standard practice; in others, it is not. At PSEG, all entry-level candidates must be tested before they are considered. Testing requirements are usually posted on the company Web site. If you are uncertain about the requirements, ask the interviewer if this is part of the interview process.

One Fortune 500 participant said the idea of testing discourages a lot of candidates who may apply for the open position just for the sake of applying, but are not especially interested in working for the company. So instead of receiving 500 resumes for one open position, a testing requirement can eliminate up to 400 résumés. The pool of applicants becomes less dense. The important thing to remember, then, is that if you are serious about the open position of a particular company, do not be discouraged by a test requirement. By all means prepare for the test and take it. If you do well, your odds of getting an interview are actually better than if you applied to a job that 500 other candidates were seeking.

ANSWERING AND ASKING

Respondents were creative when the topic of questions was addressed in the survey, so several chapters of the book are devoted to the questions (as well as the answers). Breaking this aspect of the interview into percentages and numbers just doesn't work. But 100 percent of the respondents said that candidates should *always* ask questions. But not just any questions. You have to ask the right questions—questions that flow organically from the conversation and pertain to the job or company. Timken's Martin said, "They should reflect genuine interest and be related to the position or the industry, not gratuitous or textbook questions."

How many questions should you ask? Sherri Martin, a director of human resources at Deere, answered that there is no limit, but you have to be "reasonable and not take over the interview with too many questions." Energy East's Lamoureux said, "The amount depends on the rapport" between interviewer and interviewee. Art Calderon, a director of human resources at Phelps Dodge Corporation, said, "The candidate should always be respectful of the interviewer's time and schedule."

An interview, ideally, is a 50-50 exchange of information. The employer is evaluating you and *you are evaluating the company*. Engelhard's Mangiarano called the interview process a "dance." Some career experts call it a "blind date." Whatever you call it, that one hour is loaded with information, emotion, reflection, and, with some good fortune, satisfaction.

According to the respondents, their top priority in hiring a candidate was the following: 28 percent said qualifications; 12 percent said experience; 16 percent said skill fit; and 32 percent answered "all of the above." A few respondents, once again, have a few priorities of their own: Office Depot's Anne Foote Collins said she looks for leadership in addition to skill fit. Barbara Morris, a vice president of human resources at Baxter International, looks for a solid track record. Deere's Martin looks at a candidate's education in addition to experience. PSEG's Garofalo said, "We hire the most qualified candidate for the position. This is a combination of education, experience, an electronic reference report, performance evaluation (for internal candidates), attendance, interview, background, and medical." Thrivent's Palmer looks for team fit in addition to skill fit.

And HSBC's Little likes team players too, but adds that applicants with a very professional attitude toward work are also desirable.

All of these attributes are probed during the face-to-face. As already mentioned, the interview may start as a pleasant conversation, but you can expect the behavioral questions to be lurking in the background. Fortune 500 hiring professionals know how to get to the heart of the matter. They are determining your workplace fitness, so it's necessary for them to quiz you on many levels that go beyond your skills and qualifications. Prepare yourself to be grilled—in a friendly manner, of course. Allied's O'Leary said candidates often stumble on "behavioral questions that ask for specific examples. Many struggle to the point that they can't give any specifics; only less valuable generalities." Many Fortune 500 respondents disclosed this is a typical question that creates discomfort in applicants: "Why are you leaving your current job?"

Employers today are looking at the whole package. Your personality matters. Only two respondents said that other factors are more important than personality. A large majority of respondents—52 percent, in fact—felt the personality of the candidate is important, and 24 percent felt it is "extremely" important. One respondent said fit within the company is more important, and another respondent considered job-related competencies more important. Of course, defining *personality* is a loose science, but one thing is certain: Your skills and qualifications are not the only criteria being evaluated at a job interview. Chapter 7, "What Fortune 500 Employers Value," should provide more detail on what employers mean when they say personality is important.

HOT TOPICS

Behavioral questions aren't the only stumbling blocks for many candidates. If there is a gap in a résumé—whether from a layoff, from having been fired, or even because of a criminal record—candidates often squirm. The Fortune 500 respondents thought candidates should be brief but honest too. You would not have been called in for an interview if they weren't interested—in spite of the gap. And so much depends on your attitude—of seeing what good came out of a difficult situation. Focus on what you learned, how you grew, what kind of contingency plans you came up with. Allied's O'Leary advised candidates to "be honest, with a positive spin on learning experience. Be able to provide positive references as a balance." And Deere's Martin said, "Never claim to be a victim. Admit to a shared responsibility but not too much detail beyond a basic explanation."

Another hot topic of conversation is salary. Overwhelmingly, the respondents agreed that this topic should be initiated by the interviewer—not the candidate. You need to pay attention to the signals, though, because this discussion can occur at various stages of the interview. Twenty percent of the respondents said they initiate the topic of salary in the telephone screen; 40 percent said they talk about money at the first interview; 8 percent reported the conversation begins during the second interview; and 8 percent said it is not brought up until an offer is made. Pay attention to the subtleties. Even if an interviewer brings up salary in a telephone screen, he or she may not talk about specifics until the offer is made. Don't think a mention of salary warrants an effusive negotiation. Pay attention to the clues. Hiring managers want to see first and foremost that you are interested in the job; money should be handled as an afterthought (even though it probably is *not* an afterthought to *you*).

The final chapter of this book covers the topic of salary negotiation. In addition to the feedback of the Fortune 500 hiring professionals, other experts were asked for input, as nearly 41 million Americans work for companies with fewer than 50 employees. That means you may have more flexibility when negotiating because salary ranges are not so rigid in smaller companies. Also, professionals in human resources are tough negotiators, so you need to have some strategies to balance this negotiating process.

The survey reveals again and again that preparation for the interview is the single best strategy a candidate has at his or her disposal. So research and then research some more. The more you know, the better your interview—guaranteed. The nine chapters that follow should arm you with the information you need to ace the interview, but you still need to know the specifics about the job, the company, the industry, and, most important, yourself.

In an article in *Esquire*, Jeff Bezos, Amazon's CEO and founder, was reported to have asked: "What characteristics do I look for when hiring somebody? That's one of the questions I ask when interviewing. I want to know what kind of people they would hire."[4] How would *you* answer that question? Maybe you would answer, "People like me." But be prepared to substantiate your answer—and you will need to know a lot about your work self to answer that question well.

Freud once said you need two things to be happy: meaningful love and meaningful work. Some of us deplete every ounce of our energy in the pursuit of love. The late-night phone calls, the long-distance tribulations, the expensive tokens, the relationship building—all in the name of love. Maybe it's time to invest an equal amount of enthusiasm and dedication in the pursuit of meaningful work. It may not be as heart pumping, but the rewards are just as substantial. The need to be useful, after all, is primal. So put your thinking cap on, invest the time, and figure out where your skills and strengths can best be utilized. Discover your work self. Rest assured, once you know that side of yourself, the offer will be made.

2

RESEARCH: THE INSIDE SCOOP

*"Do your homework. Study the ad or posting and prepare notes
on your relevant experience. Be prepared to provide specific
relevant examples with quantifiable results."*

KATHY O'LEARY
Manager, Employment Services
Allied Waste

Many of you will spend a lot of time thinking about what you are going to wear to your favorite cousin's wedding, or which French restaurant you are going to dine at on the weekend, or how to pay your credit card bill by Thursday—but refuse to even entertain a thought about what you want to be doing professionally the next time an opportunity or need arises.

It's not unusual to avoid this subject. Perhaps it has something to do with some nebulous fear of rejection or failure; perhaps it has something to do with that preoccupation with the daily business of living; perhaps it has something to do with tuning out the messages your parents and teachers inundated you with as you embarked on a new career, or perhaps it's simply a matter of adhering to a philosophy of life that urges you to live in the now.

There can be any number of reasons why you don't want to think about your professional future, but, in reality, it makes far better sense to discard the old habits and instead set aside some time to thinking—and planning—your next career move. Let's face it, a good portion of your time on this earth will be spent making a living. Maybe it's time to ask yourself whether you want your career to be fulfilling or whether you are willing to settle for any job that pays the bills.

You may be asking yourself what all this has to do with a job interview. You already have the coveted meeting next week, so you want to hear about the questions or the negotiations—or what to do in a face-to-face with HR or whether it's appropriate to jot down some notes. What's the point of research when you are so close to landing a job?

Interviews are made up of questions and answers. In their simplest form, the interviewers ask you questions, and you answer them. Then you ask the interviewers a few questions, and they answer them. There are times, especially in behavioral interviews, when you have to think on your feet and talk about something completely unrelated to the position, but your research now should still form the basis of most of your questions and answers.

Everything revolves around knowing what you want to do and how you can offer your skills and services to an employer. According to Richard Bolles, the author of *What Color Is Your Parachute?*[1], the best interview is a 50-50 exchange of information. It is all about the give-and-take. In a job interview you are being evaluated, but you are also finding out if the job is right for you. You need to know a lot about the company you are planning to work for, and you need to know a lot about yourself. So take the research process seriously. You are building a career and a reputation—not settling for anything that comes along.

SETTING YOUR EYE ON THE TARGET

Even though your livelihood has a direct impact on your personal happiness, most people never fully address their career prospects. In a recent book, *The Rhythm of Life: Living Every Day with Passion and Purpose,*[2] Matthew Kelly, an Australian author and lecturer, wrote that when he surveyed 40 graduating seniors, only 1 had a specific plan for achieving his goals. The remaining 39 students told Kelly about their vague wants and befuddled desires—and didn't have a clue how to go about implementing these fuzzy ideas into their own life.

Obviously, as you are reading *You've Got the Interview... Now What?* and probably have thus already examined other materials, you are in the process of developing a strategy for achieving your goals, but be careful not to rush past the preliminaries. In the predecessor to this book, *Get the Interview Every Time,*[3] one word the Fortune 500 HR professionals used consistently was *target*. Hiring managers stressed again and again that job seekers should eliminate the superfluous (and the mass mailings) and instead target their résumés and cover letters to specific job openings.

Most likely, if you have tweaked your cover letter and résumé to perfection and have garnered the interview, it means that you have presented yourself to a company as a good fit—your skills match their needs. But to ace the job interview, you need to know two things: (1) what you want to do in your next job and (2) exactly what you have to offer a specific company.

Even if you are capable of putting on a spectacular performance and securing a quick job offer, it still makes more sense to do your homework before the interview. Research saves you a lot of wasted energy and unnecessary grief by helping you to find out ahead of time if the prospective job is going to be the fit that works for both you and the company.

HOW TO START

As previously mentioned, it all begins with research. Fortunately, in an online world, access has never been easier. Every Fortune 500 company that participated in the survey for this book has a comprehensive Web site that provides job applicants an inside look. You can find out everything from a company's tuition reimbursement program to whether it offers its employees a 401(k) plan. But before you even look at the career page of a company Web site, it's a good idea (especially for newcomers to the job market) to assess your skills and then study your industry.

To make a good match, you need to know something about yourself as well as something about the job market, so at this point, ask yourself a few of these questions.

- Do you know what skills you prefer to use throughout the course of a day?
- Do you know what kind of contribution you want to make on a day-to-day basis?
- Do you prefer working for one boss at a small company or are your skills going to be most appreciated in a team-oriented atmosphere at a large corporation?
- Do you want to work for a service-oriented nonprofit or are you zeroing in on a big Fortune 500 company?

If you already know the answers that relate to your own skills and strengths, what about your industry?

- Do you know what the average salary range is for someone with your experience?
- Do you know how much education is necessary to meet the requirements of the job?
- Do you know what skills are necessary to perform the job you are applying for?
- Do you know what the latest trends are in your industry?
- Do you know which technology skills are most valuable in your profession?

Perhaps you answered these questions even before you wrote your résumé and cover letter. That's a good indication that you're on the right track. If these questions stumped you, then you probably are not ready to go on a job interview. Sherri Martin, a director of human resources at Deere, said this is the question that applicants stumble over most often at a job interview at her company: "What provides you with job satisfaction?" It seems a simple enough question, but it's one you won't be able to answer convincingly if you haven't given it some thought and done some research.

COLLEGE CAREER CENTERS

Nearly every college and university has a career services center devoted to setting its students on the best career track. These centers provide assessment tests and help students gather information and develop résumés and cover letters, and even allow them to participate in mock interviews. According to Chrystal McArthur, associate director of career services at Rutgers University, it's not unusual for job seekers to overlook this valuable resource. She claims that almost "50 percent of students don't know what their next [career] step will be."

Many of you may have taken advantage of this type of resource at college when putting together your résumé and cover letter, but, according to McArthur, the career process is more complex. Counselors at Rutgers Career Services prefer to work with students during the entire course of their studies so they can build a solid relationship that will help students discover all their options. McArthur explained, "Throughout the four years, there are different issues that crop up. Some students come in and say, 'I don't know what to major in,' or some students say, 'I need help getting an internship,' or some students say, 'I need help with my résumé.' We get a lot of students who come in senior year who have not thought at all about what they want to do when they leave. In addition, the people who are even more challenging are those who have had no preprofessional internships. Maybe they have worked at McDonald's or Gap."

Even if you have some catching up to do, don't be discouraged. McArthur said that much "depends on the person." She explained that students who are "diligent and self-reflective in this collaborative process" can discover their strengths and skills fairly quickly through a variety of tools used by the career center. One student, a business major who came in requesting help with her résumé just before she graduated, discovered after four sessions that she was better suited for a nonprofit organization than for corporate America. After taking an assessment test (John Holland's Self-Directed Search) and then sitting down and talking with her counselor about her interests, favorite classes, leadership skills, grades, and strong commitment to service, the student shifted her job search significantly.

"We're trying to put a puzzle together," McArthur said, and career centers have many tools at their disposal to help students discover and identify their strengths and skills. The Holland Self-Directed Search or assessment test (McArthur prefers to call it an "assessment instrument" because there is no such thing as a right or wrong answer) operates on the concept that "birds of a feather flock together." She said that Dr. John Holland's "research has shown that people have certain likes and dislikes. If you're in a work environment where your values, skills, and interests are fairly consistent with the group's, then it's more likely that you'll like your work."

Although the service for students is free at college career centers (usually extending three months to a year after they graduate), alumni can also benefit from these career centers. Rutgers charges $40 an hour for personal career counseling.[4] For alumni thinking about changing careers, the University of South Carolina offers special packages. For instance, for $120, alumni can get two one-hour counseling sessions and one half-hour session that include a "Strong Interest Inventory, a Myers-Briggs Type Indicator [another psychological assessment instrument], test interpretation and follow-up, access to career guidance software, and use of the Career Library resources."[5] The Career Exploration Service at Ohio State University offers various packages to members of its alumni association, such as the Buckeye Career Assessment Package for $100, which also includes the Myers-Briggs Type Indicator and Strong Interest Inventory as well as a session with a facilitator.[6] In fact, most colleges and universities actively reach out to their alumni through the career centers.

In addition, these sites are a networking gold mine for alumni. At the University of Nebraska (Lincoln), an Alumni Advisory Network encourages alumni to assist, coach, and support other alumni—both professionally and socially. Not only does the UNL Career Services have a "Husker Hire Link" that connects employers and alumni but also offers a "lifelong career assistance" program.[7] At the University of California (Santa Cruz), the online alumni association has a mentoring program through which students or alumni new to the workforce or changing careers can hook up with a mentor to gather information.[8] The Alumni Career Network at the University of Oregon assists alumni "seeking to enhance their career goals as well as those pursuing new professional interests" by matching alumni with two professionals in their desired fields.[9]

Some colleges and universities even offer credited classes to juniors and seniors that help familiarize them with the realities of the current job market. At Bowling Green University, Jessica Turos, career center assistant director, teaches a class (UNIV 331) that helps students with their résumés and cover letters, prepares them for interviews, and uses other techniques to aid students in building their skills and confidence.[10] There are also countless workshops, such as the ones offered by career services at the University of New Mexico, where topics such as "Dining Etiquette," "How to Work a Career Fair," and "Network Skills with Reception-Mixer" are covered.[11]

Make every effort to use the career center at your school because the more information you gather about the job market at the onset of your job search, the better your strategy and presentation will be when you eventually interview for a job.

But what if you are not a student or alumnus? Just go online and explore the Web sites at several colleges and universities. You won't get the personal attention students or alumni would, but these Web sites provide invaluable career guidance. In fact, a plethora of information is available—everything from worksheets that aid you in identifying your transferable skills to questions you should ask at an interview. Even more important, research on these sites furthers the "self-reflective" process: You actually start to think about your individual skills and strengths, which helps you to develop a mind-set that comes across as focused and prepared in a job interview. You have done your homework, so you know what you want and you know what you have to offer.

STATEWIDE EMPLOYMENT SERVICES

Another option is to research the statewide employment Web sites that offer training and placement as well as industry trends in a specific area. For instance, on the Massachusetts Division of Career Services (http://www.detma.org),[12] you can find a wealth of material on organizing your job search, identifying and learning to talk about your skills (they even provide scripts), finding new sources for job leads, preparing for job interviews, and tips on how to decide if a job is the right fit for you. The CareerZone, featured on the New York State Department of Labor Web site, is "an interactive career exploration tool that . . . provides information about the skills and education required, the tasks involved, and the job outlook and expected wages for any of the careers selected. You can then link from the job title to current job offerings in the New York Job Bank."[13] New York state residents can even take an assessment test free of charge on the O*NET Interest Profiler.[14] Every state has an employment services site, so investigate the Web site of the state where you plan on securing a job.

SURFING TO SELF-DISCOVERY

Why would you explore these Web sites if you already have garnered an interview? Because the more you know about what you want to do, the easier it is to convince an employer that you can actually do it. In addition, to make a persuasive pitch you need to know the language of the place where you want to work. Think of it this way: every time you research these sites, you subconsciously pick up the words and phrases that are apropos to the current work environment. You find out what skills are in high demand, and you figure out how you can transfer what you already know to what is required at the prospective job.

Then there are Monster.com, WetFeet.com, and Hotjobs.com, to name three of hundreds, perhaps even thousands, of online job sites. These sites are primarily job banks, but you can also find salary information, interview techniques, and even information on how to plan a relocation. Surfing these sites on the Net is a good way of getting to know your work self. This is especially true for newcomers to the job market or sequencers (those who have opted out of the workforce to care for others for an extended period). Time spent surfing through job banks can bring you up to speed on current expectations in the workplace. In addition, employers expect everyone to navigate the Internet with ease. According to one Fortune 500 hiring respondent, the most egregious mistake a candidate can make when interviewing is to lack information about the company. The HR director said, "In this day and age, if you don't have access to the Internet, well, where do you come from? The moon?" Set aside some time and go to the library if you don't have access at home or at the workplace.

Many of the HR professionals who participated in this survey said you should "be yourself" at a job interview. Obviously that doesn't mean showing up at an interview in your comfortable clothes with a laundry list of requests and demands—even if that's a palpable version of your real self. Rather it means knowing who you are as a worker and what you can offer the company.

TRANSFERABLE SKILLS

So far, this chapter has focused on doing research so you can explore more fully your strengths and skills. Because *You've Got the Interview . . . Now What?* urges you to move away from fuzzy goals and instead aim your research so it reveals exactly what you want and what you have to offer, it's necessary to go into some detail here about exactly how to translate strength and skills into "quantifiable" (a word frequently used by the Fortune 500 respondents) results.

Still perplexed? You are not alone. In *What Color Is Your Parachute?*, Richard Bolles devotes an entire chapter to the subject of *skills*, because "there is a total misunderstanding of what the word means."[15] He further explains, "By understanding the word, you will automatically put yourself way ahead of most job hunters." Bolles calls your transferable skills "the most basic unit—the atoms—of whatever career you may choose."

So what are transferable skills? Remember when you created your résumé and used that list of "active verbs" to describe yourself (for example, *organized, structured, researched, managed, supervised, mentored, programmed, streamlined, administered, persuaded*)? Those verbs describe the skills you have acquired—not just at your last job but in all your activities. If you went to school, you *researched, wrote,* and *edited* reports. Those are skills you bring to the workplace, where, most likely, you will be expected to research, write, and edit. Even if you are one of those "challenging" students who has little preprofessional work experience other than waiting on tables at the neighborhood restaurant, you still developed transferable skills because you *juggled* multiple orders, *provided* excellent customer service, *built* a loyal clientele, *coordinated* and *delegated* tasks. In fact, you can turn practically all of your life experience into transferable, marketable skills once you learn how to identify them.

Newcomers to the job market, sequencers, or those who are changing careers usually have the most difficulty identifying their skills because they have not yet adopted the language of their new profession or they are still uncertain what transferable skills they have to offer a new employer. That's why research at this point is so invaluable. Take a look at the "Skills Search" link of the Occupational Information Network,[16] which lists six skill groups (Basic Skills, Complex Problem Solving Skills, Resource Management Skills, Social Skills, Systems Skills, Technical Skills), to see how you can translate your experience into these marketable skills.

Cataloguing and comparing your skills with the Occupational Information Network's list of skills is not a labor-intensive exercise. It's basically a checklist that helps a job seeker identify his or her experience in language that employers understand. For instance, if you had to decide how your club was going to spend the money it raised at a recent benefit, that skill would translate fairly easily into a resource management skill. If you helped everyone in your dorm hook up to the Ethernet, then that's a useful skill that fits into the Occupational Information Network's technical skills category ("Installation—Installing equipment, machines, wiring, or programs to meet specifications").

If you are still struggling to figure out where to apply your skills, then take a look at the article on Quintessential Careers, "Strategic Portrayal of Transferable Job Skills Is a Vital Job Search Technique," by Katherine Hansen,[17] or go back and review some assessment tests available online. The Princeton Review Career Quiz is free and relatively simple: just press the radio buttons and answer the 24 questions. In a few minutes the test provides you with a general idea about your interests as well as your working style—and that helps streamline your focus.[18] If you want to invest more time and funds, then take a look at the "Online Career Assessment Tools Review," featured in Quintessential Careers's (www.quintcareers.com) "Career Assessments Section." It rates all the tests—everything from Holland's Self-Directed Search ($9.95) to the Career Test by CareerFilter (a hybrid of the Myers-Briggs test [$14.95])—and gives enough detail so you can determine which specific test is right for you. None of the career tests rated in this review costs more than $30.[19]

You already have an interview, so why bother? It's simple. Even though you wouldn't have been asked to come in for an interview if you didn't match the company's skill fit, the ability to effectively communicate these skills to the employer at the interview is essential. In fact, Allied's Kathy O'Leary suggested that at her company, which employs 26,000 people, you should "prepare notes on your relevant experience" so you can address this topic at the job interview.

For those who have spent some time in the workforce, identifying your skills is somewhat easier as most companies periodically review your performance. The language for identifying your skills, in other words, is already in place. In "Keep Track of Your Value to the Company," Anita Bruzzese, a business columnist for Gannett News Service and the author of *Take this Job and Thrive* said, a "performance evaluation can also serve as a chance for employees to tout successes, showing their value to a company and how they met or exceeded goals." [20]

It's a good idea to keep a hard copy of all your performance reviews and then take a look at them before you go on a job interview. That way your accomplishments will be fresh in your mind (maybe you forgot about the $4,500 you saved your department when you streamlined its accounting procedures ten years ago). That goes for any variation of the performance review, whether it's a 360-degree review or a simple memo your boss sent to her boss the last time she secured a salary increase for you.

Other useful materials that address specific skills and competencies also add value to your interview. Bill Vlcek, a manager of strategic staffing at International Truck & Engine, said his company's standard interview questions are based on the Lominger 67 core competencies. What are these 67 core competencies? They are part of Lominger's Career Architect®, an HR tool for developing leaders.[21] Vlcek said there are "a set of questions that each competency comes with." The 67 core competencies were developed to decipher the qualities necessary for leadership. International Truck & Engine chooses eight to ten competencies and applies them to specific positions. Review the following 67 core competencies:

Even if you are not interviewing for a management position, keep these competencies in mind when you review your past work or academic experience and familiarize yourself with the language of workplace competency.[22]

Action-oriented
Dealing with ambiguity
Approachability
Boss relationships
Business acumen
Career ambition
Caring about direct reports
Comfort around higher
  management
Command skills
Compassion
Composure
Conflict management
Confronting direct reports
Creativity
Customer Focus
Timely decision making
Decision quality
Delegation
Developing direct reports
Directing others
Managing diversity
Ethics and values

Fairness to direct reports
Functional/Technical skills
Hiring and staff
Humor
Informing
Innovation management
Integrity and trust
Intellectual horsepower
Interpersonal savvy
Learning on the fly
Listening
Managerial courage
Managing and measuring
  work
Motivating others
Negotiating
Organizational agility
Organizing
Dealing with paradox
Patience
Peer relationships
Perseverance
Personal disclosure

Personal learning
Perspective
Planning
Political savvy
Presentation skills
Priority setting
Problem solving
Process management
Drive for results
Self-development
Self-knowledge
Sizing up people
Standing alone
Strategic agility
Managing through systems
Building effective teams
Technical learning
Time management
TQM/Re-engineering
Understanding others
Managing vision and purpose
Work/life balance
Written communications

RESEARCHING THE COMPANY

Once you have determined who you are and what you have to offer an employer, then you are ready to move to the second stage of your research: investigating the company you want to work for. Because you already have an interview scheduled, a large part of your research time between now and then should be spent on the company's Web site—and not just the career page. Sheri Lamoureux, a director of human resource planning at Energy East, said that one of the most egregious mistakes an applicant can make when interviewing at her company is to display a "lack of knowledge [about the company]." Lamoureux asserted that positions at this energy services and delivery company, which employs more than 6,000 people, are offered to individuals who demonstrate "proactive orientation." She explains: "We have some people who interview and they did not even take the time to go on our Web site to get some basic information about our company. That just tells me that they are lacking initiative—a competency we look for in candidates."

Most companies today have extensive Web sites brimming with information, so a good way to begin the second stage of your research is by looking at the career posting for the particular job you are about to interview for—whether you heard about the job through a classified advertisement or from a close friend who works at that company. There's more information contained in a brief job posting than you may think.

Take, for example, this job posting for a dividend specialist at Morgan Stanley:

Analyze, research and resolve differences resulting from dividend processing. Monitor and reconcile dividend house accounts and control receivables and payables. Assist management as required with daily processing, client queries and ad-hoc projects and assignments. Document formal procedures. **Skills required:** Dividend subject matter expertise encompassing standard processing routines, including DTCC, SIAC and Euroclear. Understanding of interim accounting, fail and stock loan tracking, claims, etc. Sound end-user computing skills. Ability to operate independently and back up the section manager when appropriate. Proactive individual who can handle multiple projects and ad-hoc assignments, interacting with colleagues at, above and below this level. **Desired:** Understanding of U.S. tax reporting (i.e., 1099s) and the implication of dividend processing on same. Ability to create workstation solutions to replace manual processes.[23]

Most likely, to even be asked to come in and interview, the applicant's résumé and cover letter already matched the skill requirements of the job (knowledge of dividends, interim accounting, U.S. tax reporting, etc.), but it is still necessary to parse the job posting so that every word it contains is understood. For instance, in the preceding posting the applicant should have some data on the companies the posting mentions (DTCC, SIAC, and Euroclear). In addition, before the interview applicants should think about the kind of "workstation solutions" they created at their last job. Applicants should certainly think about their interaction with colleagues "at, above, and below" them at their last job. They should also think of past situations in which they were proactive, independent, and adept at multitasking. If certain skills are mentioned in the posting, then you're guaranteed these skills will surface during the interview. Finally, it is fairly obvious that a few soft skills are also required—someone loyal, calm, analytical, and capable of taking direction from a supervisor. These are skills that applicants want to emphasize at the interview, even if questions about them are not asked directly.

Once you discover everything you possibly can about the position being offered, then you should explore the entire career site of the company you want to work for, and don't forget to take notes. You don't want to ask a throwaway question about whether the company has a tuition reimbursement plan if it is already explicitly described on its Web site. Your questions at the interview should be delving and incisive—not a rehash of the information readily available elsewhere.

When Bill Vlcek of International Truck & Engine was asked what personal characteristics of the job candidate are important to him, he replied that his company had "seven guiding values," which he named: respect for people; customer focus; relentless pursuit of quality in all we do; speed, simplicity and agility; innovation; accountability; and communication. These values can also be found on the careers page of the company Web site. Imagine how much more effective your responses would be—and what a better match you would be making—if you knew ahead of time what was most important to the company. Many company Web sites provide invaluable recruitment information. Not all companies have Web sites that are this comprehensive, but some company sites provide detailed information regarding what to expect at a job interview at their particular company. Take a look at "Preparing for Your CarMax Interview" on CarMax's career page for useful guidelines that are applicable at almost any job interview (see http://www.carmax.com/dyn/companyinfo/careers/interview.aspx). The Alltel career page,[24] which is also comprehensive, actually gives applicants a step-by-step rundown for the interview process:

> The first interview may be conducted by phone, in person or by video-conferencing. It may be conducted by a recruiter, hiring manager or a group of hiring managers. Once the first round of interviews is completed, the top candidates are scheduled for a second interview. Some of our positions may require only one interview while others may involve three to four interviews.

In an Internet column by Nick Corcodilos, "Ask the Headhunter," Corcodilos likened the job interview to an "open-book test."[25] This is an apt description of how you should consider—and approach—your interview. Obviously you are going to gather more information than you could possibly use at an interview, but this information gathering is a testament to your preparation skills—and should convince the interviewer that you are indeed serious about the company. Know as much as possible about the position and company before you shake hands and introduce yourself.

Moving beyond the career pages, you may want to investigate other basic information pertaining to the prospective employer. Heather Otto, an employment manager at Jabil Circuit, advised that an applicant's research should include general information about her company, which employs nearly 34,000 people. Job applicants should "look at the customers, number of employees, locations, etc." Although you may not always get an opportunity to display everything you know about the company or the industry, this basic information should be on the tip of your tongue in the event that one of the interviewers at the prospective company asks a question such as, "Why do you want to work at this company?" If you respond with hard facts to this question—rather than, "Because Company Z has great benefits"—then your chances of getting an offer improve exponentially.

For more in-depth information about a company, go to the investor relations page on its Web site. Many times the company will send you an annual report just for the asking; on some company Web sites you can view the complete annual report.

What can you find out about the company in an annual report? Because an annual report is written for investors, much of the focus is on the company's financial position, but you can also discover a company's recent business developments (for instance, in Comcast's 2003 annual report,[26] its 2002 acquisition of AT&T's broadband business is mentioned), who the division executives are, its market share, and what new products are being developed.

Another useful link to visit for online annual reports is www.irin.com, the Investor Relations Information Network site operated by DST.[27] The Investor Relations Information Network (IRIN) offers "a single point of reference" for accessing electronic annual reports. More than 11,500 current and historical annual reports are available. If you want a hard copy of an annual report, IRIN will forward your request to the company. If you are researching multiple companies, this link will save you some time, although once you have garnered an interview, you still want to go directly to the company Web site to get additional information specifically about that company.

Another tool is Hoover's Online (http://www.hoovers.com).[28] If you get a call from an HR representative asking you to come in for an interview the following day, this site is particularly helpful because it gives a brief overview of the company free of charge (subscribers have access to more detailed information). The overview provides information on the nature of the company's business, the number of employees, its top competitors, the company's rankings, and its key people as well as information about its subsidiaries. Hoover's provides a quick overview in a few paragraphs, so it's a good resource if you are in a rush, but it can also supplement your other research. Take a look at this site, even if you are not hurried.

PULLING IT ALL TOGETHER

Naturally throughout your research, you have kept copious notes on the targeted company. Use the following checklist to make sure you have covered the basics:

- Products or services the company offers
- Size of the company
- Names of the company's competitors
- Company's rank in the industry
- Information about the industry
- Company type (public or private)
- Key people
- Relevant information pertaining to your particular position

These notes will prove indispensable because not only will your answers to the interviewer's questions be informed and thoughtful, but you will also develop your interview questions from this research. Art Calderon, a director of human resources and strategic at Phelps Dodge, asks applicants to describe their "wow factor" to him at an interview. What are the components of "wow"? It's one part enthusiasm, but the other part of the mix is definitely knowledge. Don't short-change yourself. As Allied's O'Leary said, "Do your homework."

THE INSIDE SCOOP

At an earlier stage in the job search, you may have arranged an informational interview. Perhaps you sat down with an old friend at XYZ Co. to ask her some pointed questions about the marketing department, or perhaps you contacted your mother's former boss at ABC Corp. to quiz him about the pharmaceutical industry. If any of those informational interviews helped garner a formal interview, then don't hesitate to contact the person with whom you originally spoke.

Assuming you had intermittent contact with this person during the course of your job search—an obligatory thank you note and perhaps a friendly e-mail apprising the person of your progress—now would be a good time to reconnect to ask for additional advice. Don't expect another face-to-face meeting, but a brief telephone conversation or an e-mail exchange may give you an edge by providing you with a more detailed scoop regarding the company culture.

At your informational interview, you respectfully quizzed the company insider by asking some preliminary questions about the company or the industry. In a *BusinessWeek* article focused on informational interviews, Michael Laskoff commented that if "you secure an informational interview, you control the agenda."[29] But now that you have a formal interview at this company, your knowledge has expanded exponentially. You have an in-depth knowledge about the company and the industry. You have done your research. All you are missing are some nitty-gritty details. Don't be afraid to ask your original contact to provide you with further information. Consider asking the following questions:

- Do you know the people I will be interviewing with?
- Do you know the people I will be reporting to if I get the job?
- Do you remember what your interview was like at this company?
- Will my three-piece suit make a good impression, or should I wear chinos and a blazer?
- Do you know anything about the job I'm interviewing for that wasn't in the job posting?
- Have there been any recent business changes that I may not have come across during my research?

Don't be afraid to ask for guidance. According to a Purdue University publication: "Generally, most people enjoy sharing information about themselves and their jobs and, particularly, love giving advice."[30] Nurture these relationships. Regardless of the outcome of the job interview, you have made this individual a part of your network, so be grateful to those who help you—and then return the favor when you are in a position to do so.

Knowledge—about yourself and the prospective employer—is the number one strategy for getting an offer. Some of you will dispute this ranking; after all, nothing beats connections and networking. No doubt, connections and networking are helpful inroads, but, believe me, it's what you know—not who you know—at the interview.

Gaining entry to a large corporation is the biggest hurdle. If you don't have a friend, relative, or associate working at the company, consider temporary or contract work there. One Fortune 500 hiring professional offered this advice: "Never turn down an opportunity to interview . . . even if it's not exactly what you are looking for. A face-to-face exposes you to a hiring manager, and maybe there's another job in the company that's perfect for you but not open at this point. Hiring managers call people back and tell them about the job. And never turn down an opportunity to work on a temporary basis. I started as a consultant at my job. It gives the company an opportunity to check you out, and you get an opportunity to look at it."

Should you go on an interview to merely practice your interview skills? No. That's a waste of time for both parties. But if there is interest in working at the prospective company, by all means jump at the chance to interview. It's one of the best ways to see if the job and company will fit.

3

THE DRESS REHEARSAL

"We sometimes bring up the issue of salary in a phone screen because you come across candidates who are very good, very interesting, and their salary is just way out of the ballpark, so we don't even bother to interview them."

SHERI LAMOUREUX
Director of Human Resources Planning
Energy East

I t is still an employer's market when it comes to hiring, so assume that for each open position you have targeted, a slew of applicants are going after the same job. Although the prognosis for future hiring is encouraging—forecasters are calling it a Goldilocks or just-right economy[1]—the overall job market is still sluggish. That means, of course, that competition for each new position will be highly competitive.

So how do you distinguish yourself? Aside from the extensive research you have done, there are still a few more bases to cover.

THE NEXT STEP

Lisa Whittington, senior director of human resources at Host Marriott, maintained that job applicants should always "think before they speak." Even if you are habitually thoughtful, sometimes a telephone call from a prospective employer can catch you off-guard. Ask yourself what you would say this minute if a prospective employer called you. Are you ready for the telephone call?

In "How to Ace the Telephone Interview," Alan Horowitz wrote that a telephone call from a manager in human resources is not a guarantee that you will be asked to come in for an interview.[2] Horowitz explained: "Jace Mouse, manager of application development at Cars.com in Chicago, conducts about 15 telephone interviews and asks only 4 candidates to come in for a face-to-face meeting."

Companies are saving time and money today by screening the pool of applicants by telephone rather than arranging for face-to-face interviews. In a recent executive survey conducted by Robert Half Technology Associates, more than half of the respondents said that "screening prospective employees by telephone prior to meeting them was very important relative to other stages in the hiring process."[3] In the Fortune 500 survey, 52 percent said they *always* screen applicants by telephone first. Once you send the news out that you are looking for a job, you should be prepared and ready for a telephone call from a prospective employer.

That may mean that it's time to change your telephone message. Your "Yo, this is Rocky B. I'm out with the guys" will not score any points with an HR recruiter, who expects you to be nothing less than the ultimate professional—even at this stage of the game. Most likely your contact information on your résumé included both a cell phone number and a home telephone number. Fortune 500 respondents said they will honor your request and call either the cell or home as indicated, but it still is wise to make sure that both messages are straightforward and upbeat. Save the long, dramatic monologues or funny one-liners for later. Instead, "Hello, this is John Byrne. Please leave a message" works just fine.

Because the average job search lasts between three and six months—sometimes longer if the market is especially tight—you might have forgotten that you sent out a résumé to ABC Corp. three months ago, in which case being prepared for the telephone screen can be a tricky matter. That's why it's a good idea to think specifically about what you want to say if and when an employer calls. You might rehearse a few sentences and repeat them to yourself periodically. Your tone should be cordial and professional. Consider the following exchange and see if you can come up with responses that are natural for you:

INTERVIEWER: Hello, this is Myles Smith from XYZ Company. I'm calling because you expressed an interest in our company.

YOU: Oh, hello. I've been looking forward to your call.

INTERVIEWER: Did I catch you at a bad time?

YOU: Not at all. I would be happy to speak with you.

INTERVIEWER: I understand you have six years' experience working in the sales department at ABC Company. Why do you want to leave?

YOU: As much as I like my current work, I think I'm ready for a more challenging position. ABC is a small, family-owned business, and, frankly, I am eager to test my skills in a bigger arena . . . .

Notice that the hiring manager referred specifically to the applicant's experience. Most recruiters and HR professionals review résumés prior to the telephone screen, so your work history is fresh in their mind. In fact, they may be looking directly at your résumé as they speak to you. That's why it's essential to know every detail listed on your résumé, which may be easier said than done, because today it's not unusual to target specific job openings by emphasizing one skill for one job opening and another skill for a different open position. The best way, then, to handle the telephone screen is to refresh your memory periodically—going through the details of your complete work history—so that *all* of your skills and qualifications are easily recalled. It's entirely possible that the interviewer is taking notes, and this information may be addressed later in the face-to-face interview.

MORE THAN ARRANGING A TIME AND PLACE

Think of the telephone screen as your first interview with the prospective employer. If there are 20 applicants for one open position, then it's the hiring manager's job to whittle away candidates at this stage of the game. The telephone screen is a perfect vehicle for doing this: In a day or two the hiring manager can drain the pool of 20 to about 4. The hiring manager has already identified the skills required for the open position, so it's your responsibility to convince him or her that your experience and skills are the right fit for this job. Most likely, the hiring manager would not have called you if you didn't meet the basic requirements of the job, but you still have to be prepared to talk about your qualifications in this conversation.

In addition, some recruiters and HR professionals may quiz you on the *cultural fit*. If the work environment is highly stressful and long hours the norm, you may be asked if an erratic schedule is amenable to you. If the atmosphere is low-key and conservative, a recruiter may try to ascertain if you will blend in well with the rest of your team. Don't be surprised if you are expected to answer a few questions regarding your work habits, such as:

- Is your schedule flexible?
- How do feel about working overtime?
- How do you react when you are faced with multiple deadlines?
- Do you prefer working in a structured environment?
- Do you function best in a team or independently?
- Do you prefer to lead or support projects?
- Which of your skills do you prefer to use regularly?

Barbara Morris, a vice president of human resources at Baxter International, said it was important to her that applicants "understand the jobs they are applying for." Knowing specifics ahead of time about the prospective position is difficult, especially if multiple job leads are being pursued simultaneously, but try to keep some notes about the jobs you have applied for. Hiring managers are deciphering your interest in the company and the position. The more focused your job seeking, the better your chances of having the face-to-face interview.

You should also know what the position you are applying for is worth and what your salary range is. Many Fortune 500 respondents said they use the telephone screen to make sure that they are in the same "ballpark" as the applicant; however, don't bring up this topic unless the question of salary is initiated by the interviewer. Salary negotiation differs from one company to the next. Sometimes it is determined (in a general way) in the telephone screen and sometimes this topic is not discussed until much later in the interview process. Rocco Mangiarano, Engelhard's director of human resources, asserted that salary negotiation doesn't take place until the final stages of the process. "You can never negotiate anything that's not offered." Instead, Mangiarano asks his "searcher"—that is, his recruiter—to ascertain that the applicant's salary range falls in line with the company's range during the telephone screen. No exact figures are negotiated until the job is offered to the applicant. The important thing to remember is that you must research what the job is worth as well as what *you* are worth (in terms of experience and skills). Then, if the matter comes up during the telephone screen, you have a starting point—and stay as flexible as possible at this stage. The best time to negotiate salary is when an offer is made.

Engelhard's Mangiarano added that, depending on the level of the job being filled, he allows a recruiter, or searcher, to conduct the telephone screen: "If we use a recruiter, then we expect him or her to do the telephone screen. And I only work with recruiters with whom I have worked for a significant period of time . . . the reason being that I like to build relationships with recruiters so they get to know me and they get to know what I'm about. They also have to understand what Engelhard is about. By the time the recruiter screens candidates, they can screen them as well as I do to make sure they will be a good fit."

WHAT DO YOU BRING TO THE TABLE?

During a telephone screen, don't be overly concerned about what the company can do for you. In the early stages of the interview process, you make a much better impression if you focus on what you can do for the company. Before you speak with a recruiter, you need to think about what you will bring to the table.

In the telephone screen, an HR representative wants a general idea about what your capabilities or strengths are. For instance:

- Do you promote teamwork and collaboration among your peers?
- Do you develop strong relationships with your customers or clients?
- Do you consistently try to improve your skills and knowledge?
- Do you have a solid understanding of technological developments in your industry?
- Do you display initiative and resourcefulness?
- Do you manage risk well?
- Do you produce results?
- Do you remain flexible and confident under pressure?

Try to think of specific instances when you demonstrated the previous capabilities—even if you displayed them as a member of the PTA. You may not have an opportunity to speak about all your strengths at this point, but you want to be prepared in the event that you are questioned.

Sherri Martin, a director of human resources at Deere, said she expects candidates to be articulate. In fact, "poor communication skills" is her primary red flag for disqualifying candidates. Because fluency with the language of the workplace does not come naturally to everyone, especially newcomers to the job market, rehearse some responses as soon as your résumé has been sent to employers. Again, examine your résumé. Look it over and talk about it—to anyone who will listen—and figure that at this point you should be able to talk for one minute about every strength you listed on your résumé.

Remember also that you are actively listening as well as responding during a telephone screen. Don't hurry to get to the sought-after time and place of the face-to-face interview. Allow the evaluation to unfold naturally. Whittington, of Host Marriot, said that "in my initial contact, I'm just trying to get a feel for how applicants conduct themselves and why they are interested in the job and how they heard about it." In the telephone screen, don't be shy about selling your interest in the job and company. Then, by all means, sell your qualifications and strengths.

THE NOISE FACTOR

In an ideal world, your initial contact with a prospective employer occurs when it is quiet and you are in a calm, thoughtful frame of mind. But more often than not, the call comes when you are catching a train or cooking your dinner or double-checking the final numbers of your department's budget. What do you do if it is absolutely chaotic when you answer the call? Calmly tell the person that you will have to call back. Then gather your wits and call back as soon as possible.

Some career experts recommend you always request calling the employer back so that you can retool your brain, but if you are fairly confident that you can speak coherently without being interrupted, then seize the opportunity and express your interest in the job. Don't delay unless you are literally jumping on a train or burning the stir-fry or in the middle of a numbers-crunching meeting with a rowdy bunch of coworkers. If that (or a similar scenario) is the case, then politely ask the employer if you can call back at a scheduled time. But in this tight job market, the sooner you reschedule the call, the better.

Host Marriott's Whittington added this: "If I have a scheduled time to talk to the person and he or she asks me to call back, I'm OK with that as long as it's something urgent that came up suddenly. It if happens more than once, I'll probably move on to someone else."

THE MINI INTERVIEW

At Jabil Circuit, a provider of electronic manufacturing services and an employer of more than 41,000 people worldwide, telephone screens are always the first point of contact between employer and job seeker. Be assured that at large companies hundreds of résumés are reviewed before narrowing the selection, so if you are one of the 15 people or so who makes it to the telephone-screening round, then you have already jumped a few high hurdles. Your résumé is obviously working for you.

Treat this opportunity seriously. Expect to answer standard questions and remember the interviewer is comparing what you say with what the other candidates have said. Always emphasize the positive, but do not get too discouraged if you don't make it past the initial phase. According to Deere's Martin, applicants should "realize that not every position you interview for will be the right fit." Host Marriott's Whittington adds, "I will tell an applicant during the phone interview that I think he or she is not a fit for the job. Sometimes something big comes out that immediately eliminates someone, and I will go ahead and tell [that person]." Regardless of the outcome of this conversation, remain cordial and professional. If you are told that you are not the right person for the job, ask to be considered for other opportunities as they come along.

Telephone screens can last more than a half hour. Ideally, there should be an equal amount of give-and-take, but realize that the interviewer is going to steer the conversation so that you answer all the questions that he or she asked the other candidates. Also remember that the initial telephone screen is no guarantee that a face-to-face interview will be arranged immediately. Occasionally, interviewers say that they need to call you back to let you know if you qualified for the next round. Stay positive. Not only do interviewers want to see if you can think on your feet, but they are also interested in how you handle *process*.

QUESTIONS TO ASK

Every job interview is a give-and-take—the questions are as important as the answers—and the telephone screen is not the exception. Consider this an opportunity for you to discover whether this job is right for you. Resist talking about what the company has to offer in terms of pay and benefits and instead focus on the exact nature of the job that is being offered. Here are a few sample questions to ask at this stage.

- When do you expect to fill the position?
- From what I have gathered during our conversation, if I am hired, I will be working for John Smith in the accounting department. Is this a newly created position or am I replacing someone?
- Can you give me a little more detail about my day-to-day responsibilities?
- How would you describe the work environment at your company?
- Provided I perform well, do you think there is room for advancement at your company?
- What major obstacles did the person who held this job previously face?
- Where is the person who previously held this position going?
- What computer technologies (or systems) will I be working with on a daily basis?
- What level of expertise do you expect me to have?
- How soon will you be conducting on-site interviews?

Take notes if you can because the telephone screen may be your first *inside* introduction to the company. Depending on how the conversation unfolds, you may be able to glean valuable information that you can use at a later stage of the interviewing process. If you cannot take notes during the telephone conversation, jot down some thoughts afterward, and try to pinpoint what the interviewer thinks is important about the open position. Chances are the interviewer's thoughts and values are a good reflection of the company's—and one more example of why it's so important to be an active listener.

GETTING READY FOR THE FACE-TO-FACE

To use the expression of Phelps Dodge's Art Calderon, you have described your "wow factor" to the telephone screener and won a face-to-face. Congratulations. The date and time for the job interview are set. Your research is complete and directions to the corporate office are exact. What do you do next?

Practice.

Without a doubt, there is a learning curve when it comes to job interviews. The more often you interview, the more adept you become; however, if a recruiter calls and asks you to come in for a face-to-face and you realize that you have no desire to work at that company after speaking to him or her, then be honest. Resist agreeing to a site interview; the following advice is from the Penn State Career Services Web site: "If you receive an offer for a site interview, respond promptly and professionally. If you are not interested in that company, decline politely. Never go on a site interview for 'practice.'"[4]

Time is precious and the job market is tight. Going to the trouble of arranging a site interview when you have absolutely no intention of taking the job if it is offered is unfair. An actual job interview is not the place to practice your interviewing skills (however, if you honestly are interested in the position and the job isn't offered to you, then it's perfectly acceptable to tell yourself that the whole exercise was good practice). Remember, you may be working in your industry for 40 or 50 years, and most industries are not as large and anonymous as you think. Your reputation as a solid, honest professional should be cultivated—now and in the future. Chances are the people you meet during the job search are not going to even remember you a few years from now, but you still don't want to make a habit of wasting people's time. For one reason or the other, bad behavior has a long shelf life, so do yourself a favor—as well as everyone else—and refrain from displaying arrogance and immaturity in your work relationships. If you plan on a long, fruitful career and a large network, then treat all your work relationships with as much respect as you would a favorite teacher or uncle. But if you are interested in the company, then by all means go on the interview—even if you are currently employed and not quite ready to move to another position. You never know what might turn up at a later date.

So to get ready for an interview, a better plan is to sit down in a quiet place (preferably when no one is home) and talk into a tape recorder. You may think you are a born speaker and talking to a dusty, archaic gadget is silly. Think again. For those who are not old hands at speaking comfortably to relative unknowns, speaking at a job interview can be an enormous challenge. For some, culturally, it is awkward to sing your praises in public. Not to mention that our everyday language is full of fits and starts—stalling techniques ("Um"), unfinished thoughts, and inarticulate transitions ("like")—that prevent us from clearly expressing who we are and what we want. That's why it's a good idea to practice with a tape recorder. A few recording sessions can help rid your speech of language tics and also help you formulate your ideas in a confident, cohesive manner.

Why should you do this? One reason is that your skill as a communicator is being evaluated during a job interview. Aside from a good personality or a good fit, a majority of hiring experts insist that good communication skills are essential. In fact, 90 percent of the Fortune 500 respondents said "poor communication skills" (in conjunction with other factors) may initially disqualify a candidate. Office Depot's Anne Foote Collins asserted that poor communication skills are one of the red flags that "would potentially be cause for pause in the hiring process." Lara Crane, a manager of staffing at Alltel, said that "many positions at Alltel are customer-facing (both internal and external). If a candidate can't communicate clearly or would not be able to build relationships among different department members, then the demands of the position will not be met as easily."

American business is geared primarily toward service (as opposed to manufacturing), so a company's bottom line depends on the ability of its workers to communicate clearly and effectively to one another as well as to its clients and customers.

Even newcomers to the workplace are expected to demonstrate this skill. In regard to recent graduates, Energy East's Lamoureux said, "The expectations for new entries is that they are not going to have a ton of experience other than potential internships, so you really are looking at their future potential. Obviously they need to have good communication skills."

According to a recent study by the National Association of Colleges and Employers (NACE), "[e]mployers responding to NACE's *Job Outlook 2005* survey were asked to rate the importance of a variety of skills and qualities.[5] Communication skills, as well as honesty/integrity, earned the highest ratings." Marilyn Mackes, NACE executive director, explained: "We've asked this question for several years, and since 1999 communication skills—both written and verbal—have topped the list." You probably have heard this emphasis on communication again and again, but you may be wondering how you can improve your communication skills immediately–or at least in time for the interview.

You can improve your communication skills *immediately* by researching the position and company, and then talking about it. Become a subject matter expert about the job you are seeking as well as what you have to offer.

Start by examining your résumé, and then use the tape recorder to talk about your skills. Listen to what you say—objectively. First consider the general impression. How do you sound? (Depressed? Positive? Nervous? Confident?) Where can you remove a "you know"? Where can you pause without losing the listener's (you, in this case) attention? Should you slow down? Should you talk faster? Then ask yourself if you are conveying your skills in a coherent and logical fashion. Are you putting too much emphasis on your routine duties and not enough on your accomplishments? Are you speaking to the requirements of the prospective job? Can you easily recall how long you were with XYZ Co. and what your responsibilities were? Can you say why you are right for the job you are interviewing for?

Going on an interview is, in many ways, comparable to speaking in public. If you think about it, you have about an hour to clearly express yourself to relative strangers. If that idea accelerates your heartbeat, you are not alone. According to Rod and Eversley Farnback, authors of *Overcoming Performance Anxiety,* "Performance anxiety is ubiquitous, and few of us escape it completely."[6] Most people— and not just the shy among us—would prefer solving a computer problem with outsourced workers on the telephone to speaking publicly about their strengths and weaknesses. That's one of the reasons why rehearsing for an interview is so important. The better prepared you are, the less likely it is that you will become tongue-tied and faint of heart.

The tape recorder exercise does not have to be painful. In fact, you might even discover a second career ("I have a pleasant voice! I think I'll become a radio announcer.") Do the recording session as often as possible before the scheduled interview, and measure your progress. After a few rounds, you'll notice the improvement. Maybe you went from mumbling to speaking clearly. Maybe you got rid of the more tiresome "ums" so only a few are left. Maybe you added some heft to your normally whispery voice. In addition, your delivery of your work history is now fresh in your mind. You have all the facts at your disposal.

THE MOCK INTERVIEW

Engelhard's Mangiarano said, "You would be surprised by how many people are not prepared for an interview." Surprised? Yes and no. It was once a common assumption that you graduated from school, went on a job interview, and then worked at the same company for a good part of your life. In fact, many people thought it unnecessary to develop job interview skills as the opportunity to use those skills came only once or twice in a lifetime. Today, though, the climate has changed dramatically. According to the Bureau of Labor Statistics, "The average person born in the later years of the baby boom held 10 jobs from age 18 to age 38."[7] That suggests you may change jobs every two years. (Other statistics indicate that members of this generation change jobs every 18 months.) In an era when frequent job change is the norm and not the exception, you would be wise to hone your interviewing skills, because you want to find a job that not only pays the bills but engages your interest. Work can be fulfilling if you know how to find and land the job that's right for you. In a *New York Times* article, Lisa Belkin reported that "40 percent of respondents were excited to begin each new week.[8] That left 60 percent who weren't quite as thrilled about it, but the minority who love their jobs are a reminder to the rest of the population of what work can ideally be."

Practicing your interviewing skills is an investment in your future. The practice session can be friendly and informal. Grab a friend and ask him or her to sit down with you and play-act the interview ritual. You might be doing your friend a favor as well. Office Depot's Anne Foote Collins advised, "Spend time up front preparing for the interview, research the company (via the Web, or, in our case, by visiting a store); have someone 'mock' interview you so you're comfortable—especially if it's been a period of time since you last interviewed."

BECOMING TEACHABLE

Now that you have mastered the recording session, what's next? Take a look at the innumerable questions listed in this book—questions that you might be asked when you sit down for your face-to-face. Write out five or six questions and then hand them to your mother, brother, husband, aunt, or friend—even your father's golf partner if he's more objective and willing to help—and request that they ask you a few questions so that you can practice your interview skills (or go to the end of the chapter and use the questions listed there). Bob Rosner, author of *The Boss's Survival Guide* and founder of WorkingWounded.com, suggests you build a mock interview around the "Knowledge, Skills, and Abilities" (KSAs) section of the job posting.[9] As you did with your own résumé, examine the job listing and specifications section and pull questions from them; however, "[i]n some organizations these job-related documents are not provided unless one asks for them." If you did not have access to the required KSAs earlier, then don't hesitate to ask the telephone screener to send them to you so that you can build relevant questions into your mock interview. If you are even more ambitious, you might ask your technologically advanced child or friend to videotape this Q&A session. (If you videotape the session, then you won't have to ask for the "interviewer's" feedback. You can see for yourself where you stumbled and squirmed.)

If the thought of sitting in front of your mother and talking about your skills and strengths makes you grimace, then look at it as a future investment in honing your presentation skills. At one time or another, everyone has an agenda that needs pushing—whether working on the assembly line or board of education.

Learning how to present yourself in a convincing manner is never a waste of time. Instead, think of it as adding another transferable skill to your briefcase or lunch pail. Talking about your strengths in this manner does not come naturally to most of us, so you need to practice. There is no way around it. Remember, though, the payback will certainly be worth the effort—in and outside the workplace.

BACK TO THE CAREER CENTERS

For those who have access to career centers, don't bypass the chance to participate in a more formal mock interview. Most career centers offer this service. They have to be scheduled, but there is no cost. Chrystal McArthur, the associate director of career services at Rutgers, said she prefers to save the videotaped mock interview for last: "I don't immediately jump into a mock interview because you want to have a relationship so that the student can hear what you're saying. If you don't have a relationship, then he or she may be defensive."

The point to remember is that the more open and willing you are while practicing interview skills, the more fruitful the exercise. Ask for feedback—from professionals and anyone else who is concerned about your welfare. Don't assume you should already know how to present yourself. We don't truly see ourselves clearly, and every skill has a learning curve. In addition, according to McArthur, "That's why we do some videotaping. You can see whether this is what you want to portray. Also based on our experience, you may need to articulate your words a little bit better. You may need to be a little more enthusiastic. We always try to give feedback. Finally, we have mock interviews with employers. The students actually have a chance to interview, and they get some positive feedback (or feedback that may spur them to change)."

THE SOFTER SKILLS

Many Fortune 500 hiring professionals interviewed for this book said they always open up an interview with small talk. Engelhard's Mangiarano said, "I have a very formal interview process and I have about 15 questions that I must get through, but the first thing I do is try and put the applicant at ease." He continues, "Typically, the first thing I ask him or her is, 'How was your trip? Was everything OK? How was the hotel?'" Neil Bussell, a group manager of business solutions at PepsiCo, commented, "The first thing you do is make the applicant comfortable in the setting. I generally do small talk to start—usually about the weather or about getting to the building. I let them settle in. Generally I start with the softer stuff." HSBC's group director, Brian Little, said, "After the usual warm-up questions, we get to the point and ask what peaked their interest in working for us. This gives candidates an immediate opportunity to display their knowledge of the company and why they are a good fit."

Obviously, you don't have to practice your soft talk skills now because you have an opportunity every day of your life to use them, but it is worth mentioning that a lot can be discovered in the soft talk. For instance, when Rocco Mangiarano asks an applicant how the hotel was, it might not be advisable to say the hotel was crawling with bugs. When Neil Bussell asks how his directions to the building were, you might not want to say that the directions were so awful that you got lost for an hour because of them. Rather, your small talk should be positive—even if you are asked about the weather and you are still shaking off the 20-degree-below-zero temperature outside—or at least be diplomatic.

Good business is about good relationships, so everything about you (even the small talk) should say that you know how to have good relationships—even if you are brilliant. So now that you are enthusiastic about practicing *all* your interview skills, here are a few interview questions you may want your sister or friend to ask you:

- What do you know about our company?
- Why do you think you are a good fit for the job?
- What was the most challenging aspect of your academic experience or former job?
- Where do you see yourself in five years?
- What is your definition of an ideal job?
- Why did you change jobs so frequently?
- Where did you hear about us?
- What made you choose this career?
- What did you learn the last time you experienced failure?
- What would your last employer say was your major weakness?
- Why should I hire you for this particular job?

Spend a few minutes answering each question and pay attention to the tone of your voice, the level of your enthusiasm, the progression of your thoughts. Even when you are asked to address weakness or even failure, try to turn your answer into a learning opportunity—one that transformed you into a better person and employee.

4

THE BIG DAY

"My experience has been that people of both genders tend to push the envelope nowadays. If I'm interviewing somebody and a guy comes in with a ponytail and earring, he doesn't have a shot. That will not fit in our environment. And this is not a stuffy environment by any means. So it just doesn't go over well. I think even if you were going to interview at a retail organization or a creative design firm, I think you should really look to the old ways of dressing yourself and grooming yourself for the interview. I think that makes a very positive impression."

ROCCO MANGIARANO
Director of Human Resources
Engelhard

The primary purpose of a job interview is to get an offer, but an equally important current running through every meeting with a prospective employer is to discover whether the job is indeed a good fit for you. The interview has to operate on both of these levels for the match to produce good results. You could say that the successful interview is a meeting of minds— with a hundred variables thrown into the equation.

If these variables concern you—and the chance of getting an offer seems comparable to winning big in the lottery—then ask yourself what you can do to improve your odds. Is getting an offer merely a stroke of good luck?

Actually, luck plays a very small part in job offers. Look at it this way: until the actual interview, you were proactive and purposeful throughout your entire search. You had a strategy. If this is in doubt, let's break the process down into the following ten steps that you took before you got the face-to-face:

1. You realized it was time to find a new job.
2. You scoured the job postings, spoke to people in your network, looked at company Web sites, examined classified ads, and read industry news to see what was available.
3. You chose several positions that ideally suited your qualifications.
4. You then revamped your résumé and targeted it to each position.
5. You wrote individualized cover letters to accompany your résumé for each position.

6. You sent these résumés and cover letters according to the protocols pre-scribed by the company or contact or recruiter (whether that was by fax, by snail mail, by hand delivery, by having your best friend hand it to his manager, or electronically).

7. You made sure your telephone messages were upbeat and professional.

8. You made a detailed list of each job you applied for (keeping a file with the KSAs [knowledge, skills, abilities] referred to in the last chapter).

9. You periodically reviewed your résumé and notes on the jobs you applied for and rehearsed a few lines to use in the event that a telephone call from a prospective employer materialized.

10. You continued to research other jobs while word spread throughout your network that you were seeking a new job.

There may have been a few variations, but the point is you already jumped several high hurdles to secure your interview. Much as you might think other-wise, your job prospects are not subject to the whimsy of the gods. You are in charge. Once you identify what job your skills and experience fit, you have a good deal of control on the outcome of your interview. In fact, one way your impact can be maximized is making a good first impression.

What are ten variables of the first impression?

1. You arrive on time.

2. You are dressed professionally.

3. You are well rested and alert.

4. You are respectful of everyone you meet throughout the day.

5. You are honest and coherent.

6. You can express clearly your qualifications for the job.

7. You show interest in the job and the company.

8. Your responses to the questions are specific and informed.

9. Your questions are relevant.

10. Your personality fits in well with the team and/or organization.

With the exception of personality, nine out of the ten preceding variables are entirely within your control. Yes, you have to research; yes, you have to practice for your interview; yes, you have to be qualified; yes, you have to show up on time and in your best attire; yes, you have to be a decent human being. These are up to you. Perhaps what is beyond your control (at this moment) is the personality factor, but remember the fit works both ways. If your temperament is generally low key and slow moving, you won't work well in a high-stress environment where everyone is scrambling to meet multiple deadlines. At Jabil Circuit, a Fortune 500 company, high energy is one of the top capabilities the company looks for in an employee. Heather Otto, an employment manager, reported that "Jabil is a very fast-paced environment. If the candidate lacks energy, this is an indicator that he or she may not be successful in our environment." But who knows, depending on how flexible and teachable you are and how much you want the job, you may choose to change a few things about yourself.

So don't be discouraged if an offer is taking more time than you like. Getting hired is not a crapshoot. The ideal job is waiting for you to fill it—when *you* are ready.

INTERVIEW PRELIMINARIES

You have heard it a hundred times: show up at the job interview neatly groomed and wearing your best business attire. This is a simple direction, but it's also often ignored. Engelhard's Rocco Mangiarano said female applicants wearing "halter tops and miniskirts" or male applicants sporting "ponytails and earrings" are not going to make the grade at his company. In this regard, Engelhard's director of human resources is not the exception. In fact, the expectation at most companies is that you care enough about the job being offered to present yourself in a professional manner.

No matter how you rationalize it, a neat, professional image matters, so it doesn't make sense to struggle with this basic premise—even if you are highly individualistic and slightly rebellious. Your individual style needs to take a back seat to your professional image when you are looking for a job. Depending on your profession, invest in an outfit to wear on interview days. *All* of the Fortune 500 hiring professionals who responded to the survey said the expectation at corporate interviews is a suit and tie for a male applicant and a suit (either pants or skirt) for a female applicant. For corporate jobs, that is the appropriate attire. For positions where a suit is not required, your appearance still matters and your clothes should be neat and pressed. Don't forget to ask if you are unsure what the appropriate attire for an interview is.

And regardless of the industry, err on the side of conservative.

Subtle colors and straight lines are best. If your budget is squeezed, no one will hold it against you if you forgo the Armani and have your old suit cleaned and pressed instead. The idea is that you need to come across as well groomed and appropriate. For female applicants who associate the word *conservative* with dreary, a word of advice from the stylish, septugenarian Yoko Ono, who was often seen in men's suits as she managed the Lennon empire: "I created a kind of outfit that made it easy for me to work. It's a male society and you have to not be totally different from them; you have to sort of use their vocabulary in some ways to deal with them."[1]

It may seem obvious, but several HR professionals mentioned that applicants occasionally show up at interviews insufficiently groomed. Granted, some events are beyond your control—maybe you have to catch three buses while a nor'easter saturates you at every transfer—but it is a testament to your problem-solving skills if you have a contingency plan to ensure that you are putting your best foot forward (even if that means a change of clothes).

For a professional image, then, you may want to check off the following suggestions before your interview:

- Fresh haircut
- Clean or polished nails
- Pressed or new suit
- Shined shoes
- Organized briefcase
- Fresh scent (easy on the perfume and cologne)
- Breath mints
- Heavy-duty deodorant
- Light makeup
- Minimal jewelry

A word to those who smoke: it shouldn't come as any surprise that attitudes have changed. A friend recently reported she was one step away from getting a job offer when she was introduced to the CEO, who promptly disqualified her because she smelled of tobacco. At Weyco, an insurance benefits company in Okemos, Michigan, a no-smoking policy that fires employees who smoke *off* the job has been put into place. Howard Weyers, the president of the company, told employees "they had until January 1, 2005, to quit; mandatory testing would begin after that, and anyone who failed would be fired."[2] Given the current atmosphere, it makes sense to consider how important your habit is. If you are anxious about your interview and you must puff beforehand, then make sure to wash your hands and pop a breath mint before showing up. Is masking your smoking habit a form of dishonesty? No, just a courtesy. If you are going to be disqualified for a job, make sure it is because you were not suitable for the position—not because you were careless. Treat the job interview with as much seriousness as you can muster. So much depends on it.

DEALING WITH PREINTERVIEW NERVES

Some anxiety before a job interview is natural. You put a lot of effort into securing this meeting, and you don't want it to be derailed because of a case of nerves. What can you do to ensure that you present yourself in a confident and convincing manner? As already mentioned, feeling prepared is one of the best antidotes, but you can also realign yourself so that you are in the best frame of mind. Here are some suggestions to consider.

- Make sure you get a good night's rest.
- Go easy on the caffeine before the meeting.
- Repeat positive affirmations to yourself.
- Listen to calming music on your way to the interview.
- Look at the job interview as an opportunity to shine.
- Welcome the challenge.
- Breathe.
- Exhibit interest in the job instead of trying to be interesting.
- Stay focused and positive.
- Know that the job is yours provided it is the right one for you.

The face-to-face interview with a prospective employer is what you have been hoping for all along—act accordingly. Smile. Because this is exactly where you want to be, try not to allow any negative self-talk tell you otherwise. The prospective employer is eager to meet you because you are, after all, solving a problem for the company, so hiring managers want you to succeed. Rest assured that they will make you feel comfortable because it is not in the employer's interest to disassemble you. In fact, most hiring managers are adept at helping you feel at ease; you can therefore trust the process.

WHAT TO BRING TO THE INTERVIEW

Perhaps you secured this interview by sending your cover letter and résumé electronically. In fact, the employer may have asked you to send it in ASCII form (to make it compatible with the company's computer system), or, in other words, plain text—minus all the fancy formatting. You can breathe a sigh of relief now. Your résumé with the bullets, boxes, and bold typeface that you converted to plain text earlier is finally going to be showcased in its original form. Now you have an opportunity to bring approximately ten copies of your formatted original to the interview. These are the résumés that are printed on your finest stationery and neatly placed within your briefcase or padfolio.

Why so many résumés? Because many Fortune 500 respondents answered that once the candidate meets with human resources, and HR believes the applicant is a good fit, then he or she sometimes moves right to the next interview with the hiring manager without another day being scheduled. That's why it's important to have extra copies of your résumé. Rocco Mangiarano said that at Engelhard applicants often go through a whole day of interviewing, and an applicant could meet with up to ten people during the course of the day.

Energy East's Lamoureux concurs: "You never know who else is going to be in the room during the interview, so you want to be able to provide one [a résumé] if requested." Jabil Circuit's employment manager, Heather Otto, added a postscript: "Bring a few copies of your résumé. You never know when another manager may be pulled into the interview."

Mangiarano added: "Typically, the way the interview works at Engelhard is that you have the first round, which is an intake process. And again, depending on the level, that may include me for fit, the hiring manager, maybe the hiring manager's boss, and some peers. If it's a senior-level job, then the second round may include a couple members of our senior leadership team. And if it's a very senior-level job, like a corporate vice president or group vice president, then I would have the applicant meet with our CEO. We can generally get through with six or seven interviews crammed into one day. And for technology people, R&D, and PhDs, we have them do a whole day of interviews separate from this process, where the applicant gives a technical presentation in front of the community of R&D scientists."

Now you know why a good night's rest is suggested. Interviewing can be a rigorous process.

Another item to bring with you to an interview is a list of references, even though most Fortune 500 respondents will not necessarily ask for them at the time of your interview. But just in case, three or four references with complete contact information (including e-mail addresses) should satisfy most employers. It is always a good idea to alert your references that you are seeking work and they may receive a call in the near future concerning your career prospects at XYZ Co. As you are giving your references a heads-up, try to ascertain if your references are in the position to promptly return the call (or e-mail) to the company (perhaps they will be away on business for several weeks or are facing a hectic schedule). That's one of the reasons why it is so essential that your references are current. According to an article in *BusinessWeek,* "Most of them must be reasonably recent: If your references are all from the '90s, what does that say about your ability to build relationships since then? Musty references are as big a red flag for hiring managers as an unexplained six-month gap in employment."[3] If you cannot pick up the telephone and contact your references today, then it's a pretty good indication that they should not be on your list.

In addition, if you bring a list of references to your interview, wait until you are asked before providing them. Sometimes the employer will ask you to send them to him or her by mail or fax after the interview. Follow the instructions—even if your neatly typed list is screeching for attention in your briefcase. According to Timken's Martin, "I would say we are flexible about references. If the candidate brings them, that's fine. If we go further in the process, then we certainly will ask for them. But not having a list is not a dealbreaker."

At every stage of the interview, follow the protocols of the company. At PSEG, references are handled differently because the entire process is electronic; you receive an e-mail from PSEG with a link that opens to a Web page.[4] This is where you enter information regarding your references. You then plug in all relevant information, including the name, e-mail address, company, professional relationship, and length of the relationship. Once the information is entered, you submit this information and launch the eReference process. E-mails are then sent to your references, who are then expected to fill out a survey, which has competency-based questions (numeric scoring) with additional space for comments. If your references don't respond, they get an electronic reminder (you may actually have to get on their case too). Once all the references respond, a report is formulated and then sent back to PSEG. (For more information, see http://skillsurvey.com/HCM_main.php.)

Obviously, references are an important component of the evaluation process at PSEG, but in the whole scheme of things, references are not the primary reason you are offered the job as most employers figure *your* references will sing your praises—regardless of your actual work history. As Englehard's Mangiarano said, "I have never talked to a reference who wasn't glowing. That's why I have the searchers do it, because they can probe more deeply than I can. It would be silly for an applicant to ever give you a reference that's going to challenge his or her good standing or good name." But it is equally important to understand that even your best reference may stumble and inadvertently blurt out inaccurate or damaging information. That's why it is imperative that you have recent contact with your references. Make sure both of you are on the same page in terms of your qualifications, skills, and work habits. If you notice any hesitation on the part of your reference, move on and ask someone else.

If you are applying for a position for which you are expected to perform fiscal duties, a company may run a credit check on you—with your permission. The Fair Credit Reporting Act allows credit reporting agencies to furnish your credit information to the employer. That's why you may want to review your credit report.

For a fee (under $10), you can get a report from Trans-Union, 1-800-916-8800; Equifax, 1-800-685-1111; and/or Experian, 1-888-397-3742.

Occasionally companies request credit reports, regardless of the nature of the position.[5] Why? The rationale is that your financial stability (or instability) can affect your performance at work (stealing or embezzlement is less likely if you are solvent). This is an area that makes some employees uncomfortable (with charges of Big Brotherism), but the emphasis these days is on transparency. If you are not an open book, some employers may assume you are hiding something. You should make sure your credit report is in order. If you don't know how to interpret your report, go to your local banker and ask him or her for your credit score (above 720 is good). Of course, if any information on your credit report is inaccurate, clear up matters as soon as possible.

In an age when negligent-hiring lawsuits are becoming commonplace, more and more employers are conducting background checks on prospective employees. What will a background check tell an employer? It tells an employer where you worked and when; where you went to school and what degree you earned; whether you've been in trouble with the law (misdemeanors are often missed but felony convictions are not) and if you have a criminal record (but not your juvenile delinquency record). If you have an interview scheduled next week and some noisy skeletons are keeping you awake at night, you might want to conduct a background check on yourself. They are relatively inexpensive (some are even free), or at least take a look at the following Web site: http://www.privacyrights.org/fs/fs16-bck.htm.[6] The survey participants stressed again and again that honesty and integrity were important attributes in prospective employees, so use your discretion but tell the truth.

Other materials to have available the day of the interview are work samples. For instance, if you are applying for a position in corporate communications, recent samples of your best writing are required. Some hiring managers request samples before the interview; others ask for them during the face-to-face. But the request for samples is not confined to creative positions. Energy East's Lamoureux said it creates a favorable impression when applicants "provide samples in a nice and neat way and bring them up in a timely manner during the interview. To give an example, during the interview we may be talking about the candidate's experience with Equal Employment Opportunity training and the candidate would show a sample of the training he or she created." So whether you have a massive portfolio, a simple brochure, or neat folder documenting your past activities or accomplishments, concrete samples add impact.

Finally, it is not likely interviewers will request your business card because they have all your contact information already, but it is acceptable to ask the interviewer for his or her business card as the meeting concludes. If the person does not have a business card to give you, make sure you jot down all necessary information so that you can compose a letter or follow-up note to thank the individual for his or her time. This is especially important if you are on a second or third round of interviews and the contact information has changed. Once again, be sensitive and follow the signals of the interviewer.

A FEW MORE PARTICULARS ABOUT THE ON-SITE INTERVIEW

Many career experts agree that it is a good idea to arrive 15 minutes before your scheduled interview. Some say it is an indication of the applicant's enthusiasm; some say it allows the interviewers to move things along if the earlier interview ends earlier than scheduled or abruptly; some say it gives the applicant a chance to get a feel for the lay of the land. My suggestion is that you arrive 5 minutes early or exactly on time. It can be disruptive to a department head if the receptionist calls 15 minutes before your scheduled appointment announcing that you are there. In addition, spending a prolonged period in the waiting room does not normally have a calming effect on preinterview jitters. Instead, listen to a tape in the car or walk around the neighborhood for an additional 10 minutes; that usually has a more soothing effect. Ultimately you must decide what works for you, but the more important point to remember is that *you must not be late* for your appointment. Tardiness is a red flag to employers. If something truly out of the ordinary occurs and you are delayed, make sure to call the contact at the company to explain that you are running late.

When you are first introduced to the interviewer, smile, make eye contact, and shake hands firmly—and wait for direction before you barge into anyone's office. You are a guest. As already mentioned, be prepared for some small talk to ease the initial discomfort. You may be asked if you want something to drink. Unless you are completely comfortable in this setting, politely decline. A cup of coffee or a soft drink will just get in the way. A job interview is not a social occasion, so instead stay focused on the business at hand—winning an offer. You will have plenty of time to share a cup of java when you land the job.

The style of most interviews is conversational, but don't let this sidetrack you. Most interviewers want to know primarily if you can do the job—not what your political opinion is. Once you are in the office and asked to take a seat, sit up straight and listen carefully. One of the most glaring red flags to Fortune 500 hiring managers is a "negative or complaining attitude," so refrain from complaining about your former job or boss. Stay positive, in fact, throughout the entire interview. Hiring managers are interested in your experience, or, as Barbara Morris of Baxter International called it, your "track record."

Some career experts suggest that before your interview, you review a newspaper or memorize an inoffensive joke to break the ice. Do this only if it is natural for you; otherwise, let the interviewer initiate the preliminary conversation. Ideally, the interview will be a 50-50 exchange of information: you respond to questions and ask your own. Try to keep this balance in mind, but don't feel compelled to take charge. Let the process unfold naturally.

VIDEOCONFERENCING

When an organization or institution initiates a nationwide or international search for a candidate, videoconferences are sometimes the method of choice (especially at academic institutions). When asked about the new technology for the interview process, however, most Fortune 500 respondents said they rely on standard methods (flying candidates in to interview face-to-face). But several Fortune 500 companies surveyed do use videoconferencing, so you may be interested in what's involved.

Videoconferencing provides a simulation of a normal face-to-face meeting by enabling people in distant locations to interact (via computer) just as if they were in the same room with you. The interviewer asks a question and the candidate responds—in real time (sort of). The problem is that several technical problems can arise. For instance, the sound/video is often delayed, which makes conversation a little awkward. Then there is the issue of setting up the equipment correctly so that full-face, eye-to-eye contact is maintained. Companies do save on candidates' travel expenses, but for those not completely comfortable in front of a camera, the videoconference can be an ordeal. As always, you must treat this meeting with an employer in the same professional manner as a real face-to-face, so wear business attire (think of your friendly TV anchorperson when choosing a suit) and be prepared to ask and answer questions.

Those Fortune 500 respondents who use virtual interviews suggested it was, at best, a cost-saving alternative to the face-to-face. TIAA-CREF's Robert Moll noted, "We do occasional videoconference interviews for distant candidates," and Sherri Martin of Deere said they use videoconferencing in "very limited instances." Another Fortune 500 participant agreed that videoconferencing can be useful, but the cultural factor must be taken into account. Her experience at Sony led her to believe that many candidates' level of discomfort was so significant that this method was rendered unsuitable. But Deb Palmer, a staffing manager at Thrivent Financial for Lutherans, said, "Since we have multiple locations, we very frequently use videoconferencing for interviews. This helps reduce travel costs for candidates and/or hiring managers."

What normally occurs when a videoconference is arranged is that you either go to a prospective employer's branch where videoconferencing equipment is set up or you contract with an outside service when a company does not have its own remote facilities. Kinko's, which has a 150-site network, also provides this service and charges a few hundred dollars per hour to videoconference. A few kinks still need to be ironed out, but as the technology improves, you can expect videoconferencing to be a more commonplace means of interviewing. If you are asked to proceed in this manner, find out all the particulars ahead of time by completely familiarizing yourself with the process before the big day. Also, it is perfectly acceptable to ask the individual in human resources for additional information regarding videoconferencing. One Fortune 500 participant said you should always ask questions if you are not familiar with a company protocol—a question regarding procedure is a testament to your "professionalism."

BE YOURSELF!

Chapter 2 emphasized the importance of knowing yourself—what you want and what you have to offer. Your research revealed not only what your skills and strengths are but also what your career expectations are and how well you fit the jobs you apply for. This self-knowledge has to be taken a step further once you get the interview, because Fortune 500 respondents emphasized again and again that applicants should be who they authentically are in order to make a good match.

The fit has to work both ways, so it doesn't make sense to say in an interview that you thoroughly enjoy writing HTML all day when, in fact, you prefer spending a good portion of your time on the telephone marketing the latest project. Try to keep your responses sincere—even if you think the interviewer may want to hear something else. Art Calderon, the director of human resources and strategic programs at Phelps Dodge Corporation, advised, "Be yourself! Anything else is unfair to both yourself and the prospective employer."

Bill Vlcek, of International Truck & Engine, makes the same point. He said, "You don't want to put something over on the company nor does the company want to put something over on the applicant, because then when the work relationship starts, it's not going to be what either party expected."

The job interview is a discovery process. You are gathering information to see if XYZ Co. is the right place for you, and the employer is asking pointed questions to decipher whether you are indeed the right person to fill the job. The temptation, of course, is to win an offer every time you interview. Many are programmed to win, but taking a job that is not right for you can be a Pyrrhic victory.

As much as you may want to get an offer, an unsuitable job can be tedious or even torturous.

And it may cost you too. "Human resources professionals and labor lawyers say that more companies are compelling employees to sign employment agreements that hold workers responsible for repaying training, tuition, and relocation costs if they leave their jobs within a specified period."[7] Usually that means you have to stay at the job (which is not a right fit for you) for at least a year.

That also means that the company should present itself in an accurate light as well. Neither party benefits when winning the interview or candidate takes precedence over a satisfactory match. International Truck & Engine's Vlcek told a story to illustrate the point.

There's an HR director who gets hit by a bus. Then she finds herself at the Pearly Gates and St. Peter says, "You know, we don't know what to do with you because we never had an HR person up here before; so I'm going to give you a couple of days to check this place out, and then I'm going to send you downstairs so you can check that place out as well." So the HR director is upstairs in Heaven for a couple of days, sitting on a cloud doing Angel things. But there are a couple of real slow days and she complains to St. Peter that there's nothing for her to do. So St. Peter tells her to go back to her cloud and do all those Angel things up there. At the end of three days, she says, "This is nice, but let me try the other place." She goes downstairs where there's this beautiful place and she sees all her friends and there's a whole lot of stuff going on. The three days are over and she goes back upstairs to St. Peter and he says, "OK, it's your choice now. Are you going to stay up here or are you going to go downstairs?" She answers, "Well, you know, I really like it up here and it's so nice and peaceful and calm and beautiful, but downstairs is more fitting to my style—the activity, the friends, and so on," so down the elevator she goes. She gets off the elevator and now everything is just the dregs of the world. She finds the devil, and says, "Hey, this is way different than it was these last three days. What's going on?" So the devil answers, "Those last three days we were recruiting. Now you're staff."

5

THE GATEKEEPER

"The personal qualities I look for in a job candidate are, first and foremost, ethics and integrity; then good communication skills, enthusiasm for the job, motivation in seeking the job, and a demonstration of potential beyond the immediate role."

BARRY MARTIN
Director of Staffing and Development
The Timken Company

You don't need to be reminded of everything you had to do to reach the point where you shake hands with the human resources professional. It was a long and labor-intensive process that began with research and will end, it's hoped, with an offer. Yet so much depends on this encounter with the company's gatekeeper. Gatekeepers are the individuals who escort you in to meet your prospective boss and peers.

HR people are practiced at sizing people up—and they usually get a good reading on job applicants in about five minutes. They have already reviewed your résumé, so they know your qualifications and general skills; thus, at the initial face-to-face you are, more or less, being evaluated for your ability to communicate and to fit in. Even though HR professionals are capable of giving a fairly accurate quick once-over, protocol still requires they spend more time with applicants to ensure that their gut hasn't steered them in the wrong direction.

A successful job search takes time. Likewise, hiring decisions are made carefully at companies. Jeffrey J. Fox, author of *How to Become a Great Boss*,[1] said, "The cost of a mishire is huge . . . To reduce mishiring costs, hire slowly and with care. The more important the job, the slower the hire. The more expensive the candidate, the slower the hire. Don't succumb to the need to fill a critical vacancy. Don't hire because you have a deadline. A mishire will create an even tougher deadline."

Hiring professionals don't ignore their instinct, but they are also committed to the entire process—interviews, background checks, recommendations, and tests. Generally, these matters take time; in fact, the larger the company, the more likely the hire will move along at a slow pace. In *Get the Interview Every Time*,[2] Cydney Kilduff, an HR director at Kellogg, said, "Big wheels move slowly."

Regardless of your urgency to find new employment, keep in mind Murphy's second law: "Everything takes longer than you think." Be patient. Hiring professionals are evaluating the whole person (not just your *curriculum vitae*). Your personality is as important a factor as your work history, so let the process unfold slowly.

According to Engelhard's Mangiarano, "We are all go-getters here, but we hire nice people—people we want to work with and with whom we share a fairly common set of values." It is fairly evident then that as much as your credentials may glitter, you won't get a shot at performing your duties unless you also have the potential to work well with others at the company. Every corporation or organization expects applicants to fit its corporate culture, and HR professionals are especially adept at knowing what it takes to fit in— both professionally and culturally.

Exactly what does *fit* mean? It means you have the skills required for the job. But, equally important, *fit* means you will blend in well at the organization—with your superior, peers, and coworkers. Companies resemble families in many ways, so the dynamics—low key versus high energy, fast paced versus sedate, team oriented versus mavericks, thin skinned and sensitive versus tough skinned and blustery—are important.

Again, it goes both ways. As much as you are in need of new employment, you can't fit a square peg into a round hole. That's why it's a good idea to look at interviews as a discovery process. Yes, you are being evaluated, but you also are doing your fair share of assessing whether this is indeed a good match for you. Your research reveals a lot about how a company works, but you, too, must trust your instinct. No matter how much your ego is flattered, if the job doesn't feel right, then continue searching until you find something that is comfortable for you.

AFTER THE FIRM HANDSHAKE

There is no denying that a good first impression is crucial to interview success. Luckily, ensuring that this impression is favorable is relatively easy.

- You dress appropriately.
- You are neatly groomed.
- You show up on time.
- You smile and look in the interviewer's eyes as you shake his or her hand firmly.
- You chat amicably until you are seated.

The rest of the interview depends on how well you pay attention to the signals and, more important, answer the questions as well as ask your own. Bob Rosner, author of *The Boss's Survival Guide* and founder of Workingwounded.com, surveyed job seekers regarding the ingredients for a successful interview.[3] The results broke down as follows:

- [Flattering] the interviewer: 2 percent
- Nothing; it's like playing Russian roulette: 8 percent
- A good work history: 18 percent
- Good answers to the questions: 72 percent

Clearly your responses to the questions matter, but don't forget that you are gathering information as you move through this process. In other words, you should be *responsive* to what you have learned along the way—taking mental notes and paying attention to what the people who work at the prospective company are saying. Partly you need to be sensitive to what insiders think is significant; and partly you need to address those issues that are important to you (concerning the job at hand and not necessarily the benefits and perks). One more reminder: this is a give-and-take process—shoot for a 50-50 exchange of information.

Barbara Morris, a vice president of human resources at Baxter International, acknowledged that after the initial introduction, mistakes that immediately hit her radar screen are candidates exhibiting a lack of energy or lack of knowledge about job and/or the company. She said these red flags are a "very close tie," and if these mistakes resurface on the second round, "No energy or the applicant did not find out more about the company, then he or she is in trouble!" So don't assume your work is done once you show up for the interview. You are still on a fact-finding mission. Stay alert.

BUILDING RAPPORT

Every interview unfolds in its own way. As much as companies try to standardize the process, a lot depends on the rapport between the interviewer and the job applicant. Try not to get too caught up on what you are going to say next. Instead, pay attention to what's going on at that moment. If the HR professional seems distracted or harried, it may be time to ask a question. If you notice that the questions on her notepad are being checked off in a routine manner, try to rescue the exchange by bringing focus to your most outstanding accomplishments. Occasionally there is absolutely nothing you can do to avoid a disqualification. The HR professional obviously knows something you don't, so trust that the decision will inevitably be the right one in the long run. This is not the right job for you.

Your first encounter with human resources may be with an HR generalist. In many companies, the generalist is responsible for staffing, training, communications, and employee relations. Generalists are thoroughly familiar with the company's HR policies, procedures, and strategies. You may have even spoken to a generalist during the telephone screen. Generalists can answer any questions you may have regarding the organizational design or overall workforce of the prospective company. Generalists often provide your first inside look at the company. If you have questions regarding the infrastructure of the company, a generalist can probably answer all your questions; however, some of the Fortune 500 companies surveyed for this book have more than 40,000 employees, so keep this in mind when you begin to delve into the specifics of a particular job. Generalists know the overall requirements of the job you are interviewing for, but for a more detailed description of your daily responsibilities, you may want to reserve a few of your questions for a hiring manager or department head.

Robert Moll, a senior HR generalist at TIAA-CREF (Teachers Insurance and Annuity Association-College Retirement Equities Fund), which employs more than 6,000 people, advised that at the initial interview job applicants need to "be prompt. Be neat. Be personable. Be prepared. Know your own background, accomplishments, dates, and something about the company and job you are interviewing for."

At this point of the interview your goal is to convince the HR professional that you will fit well into this organization and that you have the qualifications to perform the job. Try to build a rapport on this level—and save the lengthy, technical diatribe on the vagaries of Java and ColdFusion for a later discussion with the department supervisor of IT.

Your first meeting with a representative of human resources is your introduction to the company, so the give-and-take will most likely open with the general and close with the specific. Keep your focus on the job being offered, and by all means allow the employer to do the steering. No matter how confident and qualified you are, the home court advantage belongs to the employer. Don't take over the interview: such a tactic is not appreciated.

THE CONVERSATIONAL INTERVIEW

For the most part, even at Fortune 500 companies, the interview is conversational—even though standard questions are often asked of each applicant. Although the style varies from one company to the next (depending on the size of the company and the level of the position), the Fortune 500 respondents said that generally their interviews are a mix of standard questions along with open-ended inquiries (behavioral based). Many respondents said they want to see if applicants can "think on their feet."

You have probably heard the expression *think on their feet* a hundred times, but what does this mean in regard to the interview? It means your input at an interview should not be a memorized script nor should you rely on stock answers. Your intuitive and analytical skills are required, so your answers must be thoughtful and meaningful. Even though questions to ask at your interview are provided throughout *You've Got the Interview,* try to remember that some of your questions should be formulated from the information that you have gathered along the way as you speak with HR professionals and hiring managers. In other words, you are expected to be *responsive* to the interview. Even good questions can seem irrelevant if you ignore what you have learned thus far at the interview. Instead, make an effort to see a connection by posing your questions at timely and relevant intervals.

TIAA-CREF's Robert Moll added: "[Candidates should] ask about four or five questions. It shows interest and preparation, but they should not ask about basic, readily available information. Instead, they should ask about the specific job, department, duties. Don't ask for the sake of asking."

Naturally, so much depends on the formality or structure of the interview. As was already mentioned, Engelhard's Mangiarano explains to candidates that they must answer his standard questions before they get a chance to ask their own. Follow directions but remain responsive to the information you have culled up to this point. You can discover much about the company by the questions the hiring manager asks.

By the time job applicants interview at Timken, a manufacturing company that makes bearings and alloy steel for everything from computers to railroads, Barry Martin knows a good deal about the applicant's qualifications, values, work habits, and level of communication skills as well as the way the applicant thinks prior to the first meeting. "The road into Timken is not the standard résumé. [Applicants] must go online and create a candidate profile in the company's new candidate relationship system."

Candidates typically visit the company site twice and interview with seven to ten people. Candidates show up for a face-to-face at the site after they have "answered multiple screening questions based on the specific roles they are interested in. We probably already did a telephone screen." For senior level roles at Timken, "general manager or above, we actually have an additional set of questions that we mail to the applicant that requires quite a lot of lengthy information—anywhere from 8 to 12 questions."

On many levels, then, the interview process has begun even before the candidate shows up for a face-to-face at Timken. Martin said that this process was implemented primarily because "not only does this allow us to see the breadth and depth of the applicants' experience, but I also get to see how they think and how they communicate." Even though the "candidate relationship system" at Timken may be time saving and cost effective, the real emphasis is on finding the most qualified candidate. Sometimes Timken can fill the position after interviewing one or two candidates but not always: "We just recently filled a Chief Learning Officer position, where we ended up interviewing, either on-site or through a teleconference, probably 30 people."

You may be wondering what is left to cover at an interview at Timken, which employs more than 26,000 people, when the screening process is so extensive. According to Martin, what he is trying to discover at a face-to-face are, in fact, two essential elements of every successful interview: "Number one, we are trying to give the candidate a good exposure to the kind of company we are and the specific responsibilities of the job along with the kind of people with whom they would be working, so that the company and the job are a good fit from their perspective. We also want to make sure they have the kind of interpersonal skills—communication skills—that are a requisite for the job."

E-RECRUITING

Wynn Casino in Las Vegas recently recruited 10,000 employees in four months, a major feat considering that more than 125,000 people applied for the open positions—from chefs to pit bosses to senior level executives—in an area that has an unemployment rate of 3.5 percent.[4] To handle the recruitment, the casino set up an employment center with 40 kiosks, where applicants (some who spoke English as a second language) went through an online screening process. The applicants were asked five questions:

1. Have you done the job you are applying for?
2. What is the level of your experience?
3. How long did you stay in your last three jobs?
4. What types of places have you worked?
5. What is your level of English competency?

Then applicants were also asked technical as well as multiple-choice questions related to the open position they applied for. The results were tabulated and ranked and became part of the overall e-assessment. Kevin Marasco, marketing director of Recruitmax, noted that "actually, over 90 percent of the applications came over the Web site. [The e-recruiting system Wynn Casino's used] had to make it real intuitive, user friendly. When the system asked for contact information, the system walked them through the process. It did this for people who are not that computer savvy, so it's real easy and intuitive. Once they get past a certain stage in the process, the system [even] says, 'OK, we need to schedule an interview.'"

Obviously, this situation is unique. Most companies do not have the need to fill 10,000 open positions in such a short time span, but you should familiarize yourself with the basics. If you plan to attend an employment fair or event, bring your résumé, a list of references, and a pocket dictionary. Make sure you are totally prepared to provide all necessary information. According to Marasco, the hiring process can unfold in a speedy fashion when a company utilizes an "electronic recruiting" system.

"First of all, the technology (we call it an *enabler*) helps [recruiters] do a better job. You're never going to replace the face-to-face interview. What the technology does is streamline the process and allow recruiters to spend more time building relationships and assessing top candidates, ultimately helping them make a better hire," Marasco added.

THE LOWDOWN ON COMMUNICATION

It should be obvious why communication skills are becoming more and more important. Not only must you know how to express yourself clearly to the people you work with every day, but now everyone is basically a writer in today's workplace. There's no hiding your lack of skill anymore. You may be saying to yourself that you are *the* premier expert in blue-laser diode development, and most likely you would prefer to spend your time working on the commercialization of blue lasers to honing your communication skills for a job interview. After all, you have a lot to offer an employer. Shouldn't the company be more interested in your development of next-generation, high-volume optical discs than how well you can express yourself to mere mortals? Yes and no.

Employers recognize talent—even if you get a little tongue-tied when introducing yourself to nine scientists sitting in on your presentation. But there is still an expectation at companies that you will be able to communicate your ideas and visions in a coherent, accessible manner. It's all about good, working relationships (of which communication is key). Add to this equation the electronic revolution—and the necessity to use e-mail on a daily basis—and the need to express your ideas clearly and concisely gets ratcheted up a notch. As is evidenced by the

Timken evaluation, you need to *speak and write* well before you are even considered a contender for many positions.

Never assume then that you can sit back on your laurels and focus on only those things that engage your interest. Your commitment to honing your communication skills must be ongoing; otherwise your opportunities for growth in your career are going to be limited. Regardless of your expertise—whether in blue lasers, mutual funds, depolymerization, HTML, or Lotus Notes—you need to communicate clearly, so attack this skill with everything you have at your disposal. In fact, commit to lifelong learning on this front. Take classes on writing or volunteer to do telemarketing for a charity—and read. Find the language you need to be an expert at your job. Whatever you do, don't settle and tell yourself that you're just a humble such-and-such—plain and simple—and not a communicator. There's nothing wrong with humility as long as it doesn't stop you from being, as Matthew Kelly said, the "best version of your self."[5]

Communicating effectively is one transferable skill that has a life of its own. In an era when the skill set changes as quickly as a traffic light, good communication skills never lose their edge. Without a doubt, there's a learning curve to sharpening these skills, but practice earns better results than complacency every time. As William Zinsser, author of the classic *On Writing Well,*[6] contends, "It's a question of using the English language in a way that will achieve the greatest clarity and strength. Can such principles be taught? Maybe not. But most of them can be learned."

I "YAM" WHAT I "YAM"

So far, two contributing factors to a successful interview have been emphasized: *good communication skills* and *fit*. It came up again and again in the Fortune 500 respondents' answers. Granted, it's a lot easier to buy into the idea of sharpening your communication skills than it is on figuring out how to fit into a company or organization. That's where the real resistance usually surfaces, but as George Bernard Shaw, the Irish playwright, critic and sage, said, "Life isn't about finding yourself. Life is about creating yourself."

As long as you don't look at yourself as a fixed entity and you are willing to be flexible, then you have a chance to be productive and engaged at a whole array of companies or organizations. It takes, however, self-knowledge and self-assessment to find out where you will fit in best. Although the topic of research was covered in Chapter 2, a slightly different angle needs to be explored in this chapter.

In your preliminary research you discovered what current skills and strengths you bring to the employment table. You looked at your work history, and you tried to arrange a good match with a company. You looked at what you did and then at what you want to be doing in the future. What you may not have considered was what motivates you.

In *Maximum Success, Changing the 12 Behavior Patterns That Keep You from Getting Ahead,* authors James Waldroop and Timothy Butler explore the psychological patterns that prevent employees from working up to their maximum potential—engaged and productive in their career.[7] The book analyzes the barriers that preclude many from realizing their full potential.

Reading *Maximum Success* will help you to better identify the root of many unconscious career mishaps, but a brief summary may help broaden your concept of work. The authors, who are executive coaches (as well as trained psychotherapists) and also directors of MBA Career Development at the Harvard Business School, claim that underlying 12 unhealthy behavior patterns are "four primary causal events":

1. A negatively distorted self-image
2. An inability to understand the world from other people's perspectives
3. Not having come to terms with authority
4. An inability to use power comfortably, skillfully, and effectively

You may be thinking that these issues are more appropriate for a shrink's couch than as preparation for a job interview. As a matter of fact, the authors' four primary causal events can actually have a decisive impact on the success of your interview. Even if you are not plagued by these "events" (a negative self-image, for instance), these are issues worth investigating as you assess what it is you want from your next job. They may also spur you to ask better questions and give more meaningful answers.

Think of it this way: If these so-called causal events are the core issues that prevent many employees from satisfactory careers (and according to the Ajilon Office study Lisa Belkin cited earlier in Chapter 3, nearly 60 percent of the working population is unhappy at work), then examining some of your own core beliefs regarding these events is worthwhile. Self-examination on this front will undoubtedly give you a much clearer idea about your career expectations and help you identify the job that is right for *you.*

If you are still doubtful that this type of exploration will avail you the results you are seeking—which, in this case, is getting hired—consider these responses from the survey. One of the primary reasons many candidates are disqualified for jobs at Fortune 500 companies is a "negative or complaining attitude." Kathy

O'Leary of Allied Waste, Mary Matatall of Continental Airlines, Sherri Martin of Deere, Sheri Lamoureux of Energy East, Lisa Whittington of Host Marriott, Heather Otto of Jabil Circuit, Robert Moll of TIAA-CREF, and Barry Martin of Timken all cited this as a primary disqualifier. Even though every career expert emphasizes that applicants should always remain upbeat during job interviews, this common wisdom has not been assimilated into the mind of many job seekers.

If you are looking for a new job, or perhaps even a new career, then it is imperative to consider the "practical psychology of being effective at work." Take, for instance, a "distorted self-image." How has this event been working in your career? In fact, ask yourself a few of the following questions:

- Do your career expectations need to be realigned?
- Do you need to revamp your attitude so that your negativity is not infectious?
- Do you always ask yourself how you can be part of the solution instead of the problem?
- Do you feel good enough about yourself to always treat others with respect?
- Do you figure out a way to build a consensus through teamwork?
- Do you remain positive or maintain a neutral position when everyone else in your group is mired in gossip and finger-pointing?
- Do you remove obstacles from the work path of others?
- Do you rally support for a project even when the position is unpopular?

The point is that the more you think about the nature of your work—and what you need to do in order to be a productive and happy employee—the better your chances are at finding a job that is suited to your talents. It is precisely this type of knowledge (and not necessarily fate or luck or even good connections) that allows you to make a good match.

In addition, *Maximum Success* lists 13 "reward values" that motivate people at work. Surprisingly, monetary reward is not always the prime factor. Why not ask yourself which reward value will be most important to you at your new job? Is it "financial gain; power and influence; variety; lifestyle; autonomy; intellectual challenge; altruism; security; prestige; affiliation; managing people or recognition"? Consider all of these values and then base some of your questions on precisely which reward value is most essential to your job satisfaction.

Equally important as you change jobs: don't forget you get yet another chance to reinvent yourself. You can toss out one or two of your bad habits—maybe your "chronic rebelliousness" or "bulldozing behavior"—and adopt some new habits that will pave a smoother road to your career goals. Today, flexibility is key, so don't resist change.

If the emphasis on practical psychology seems diversionary, then it should be mentioned that 90 percent of the Fortune 500 respondents said that the personality of the job applicant was either an "extremely important" or "important" factor. You might be wondering what you should do if you have a tendency to wear your melancholy on your sleeve. As the Fortune 500 respondents asserted, "Be yourself" at an interview, but make sure it's your *best self*.

Figure out what it takes to do the job being offered and be willing to adapt yourself to your job and your surroundings. It doesn't require a complete overhaul of your personality—just a willingness to be flexible. Investigate those underlying currents in your personality so you can make an informed decision about a job offer: a decision based on who you are, what you have to offer, and how well you can (if you want to) fit into the company.

For those who think this is mere psychobabble, a study by Right Management Consultants cited by Anne Fisher may convince you otherwise. According to the study, "About 35 percent of managers who change jobs fail in their new ones and either quit or are asked to leave within 18 months." Anne Fisher, the workplace columnist for *Fortune* magazine, said that "most managers who blow it have fine technical skills but stumble over the softer side—fitting into the culture, navigating the political landscape, and forming the kind of friendships that help get things done."[8] Your personality matters. Translate Mangiarano's "nice" people into those who are capable of building and maintaining solid relationships. It inevitably always comes back to good relationships.

Besides fit and communication skills, another theme that cropped up repeatedly in the Fortune 500 survey was a candidate's "integrity." Rocco Mangiarano of Engelhard, Kathy O'Leary of Allied Waste, Barbara Morris of Baxter International, Mary Mattatal of Continental Airlines, Sherri Martin of Deere, Bill Vlcek of International Truck & Engine, Robert Moll of TIAA-CREF, Barry Martin of Timken, and Steve Duea of Harley-Davidson made a special point to list "integrity"—or a variation thereof ("honesty" or "ethics," for instance)—as a desirable attribute.

Recent corporate scandals at individual companies have had an across-the-board impact. When Timken's Barry Martin was asked about this newfound emphasis on a candidate's moral fiber, he replied, "We are a 106-year-old company that is known for its ethics and integrity, but . . . a lot of these scandals have made companies more aware about the kind of company they are keeping. I am sure [hiring managers] ask about these issues with considerably more frequency than they have in the past."

In light of recent events, then, it should come as no surprise that your ethics may in fact become a topic of conversation at a job interview, so if you haven't thought about how your integrity impacts your job performance, maybe it's time you did. Engelhard's Mangiarano said that after he asks job applicants his standard questions, he usually ends the interview with precisely this type of question: "I ask them to explain to me a situation where their business or personal ethics were challenged. And I ask them to describe that and how they responded to it. If they tell me that their personal or business ethics were never challenged, then I know they are lying to me."

Big companies spend millions of dollars to guarantee that their name—or brand—is held in high esteem. In this type of business climate, your integrity as an employee matters, so count on a few questions at your interview that deal explicitly with this topic. Whatever you do, remain honest throughout the entire interview process, even about difficult subjects. Allied's O'Leary said the best way to handle these difficult questions, such as being fired, is to "be honest but with a positive spin on it as a learning experience. Be able to provide positive references as a balance." If you can't avoid addressing your own personal skeletons at a job interview, then manage them honestly and diplomatically—and as quickly as possible. With Mangiarano's comment in mind, it's a good reminder that everyone, at one point, has been ethically challenged. So answer these questions if you can do so honestly by focusing on what you learned and how you grew.

On the flip side, a new study sponsored by 24 leading U.S. companies and based on the responses of 7,718 American workers (the "New Employer/Employee Equation Survey") states that 54 percent of workers question "the basic morality of their organizations' top leaders and say that their managers do not treat them fairly."[9] This could be an area of investigation you may want to pursue at the interview as well. Resist using the third degree, but by all means ask the hiring manager questions about the company's policies, such as:

- Would you characterize the workforce at XYZ Company as diverse?
- How does this company resolve a personality conflict between a manager and a subordinate?
- Are your employees generally dedicated and loyal?
- Do your managers overwhelmingly care about the fate of the organization?
- Do employees generally feel passionate about their work at this company?
- How are decisions made at the company?
- Is fairness a priority?
- Is customer satisfaction the driving force?
- Conflicting viewpoints are common in organizations. Where is some of the potential conflict that I may face in my new role? How was it resolved earlier?

You don't want to find yourself among the "substantial numbers of employees [who] feel dead-ended and are seeking changes at work or new jobs altogether." The interview process must go both ways for a good match to be made. Working for a company with high standards—one based on ethics and integrity—should be a priority for you as well.

"STOPPERS AND STALLERS"

As mentioned in Chapter 2, Bill Vlcek, of International Truck & Engine, said many of his interview questions are based on Lominger's 67 core competencies. Vlcek quizzes senior-level candidates to see how they rate on core competencies, such as approachability, intellectual horsepower, and conflict management (see Chapter 2 for the complete list). But in addition to these competencies, Lominger has also created a list of "19 stoppers and stallers" to a career. Take a look at the following pitfalls and see if you need to address any of these issues before starting your new job—regardless of whether you are a customer service representative or senior vice president:

Unable to adapt to differences; poor administrator; overly ambitious; arrogance; betrayal of trust; blocked personal learner; lack of composure; defensiveness; lack of ethics and values; failure to build a team; failure to staff effectively; insensitive to others; key skill deficiencies; non-strategic; over-dependence on advocate; over-dependence on a single skill; over-managing; performance problems; political missteps.

Even though these stoppers and stallers were developed with upper management in mind, such defects are not attractive in any employee. Don't exhibit these tendencies when you are interviewing but instead focus on what you know is valuable to employers. Pam Hill, a staffing and planning director at CarMax, suggests that job candidates apply the four Es when interviewing. She recommends:

1. *Energy.* Show good energy during the interview. Don't slouch, sit up straight, walk at the pace of the interviewer, and so on.
2. *Enthusiasm.* Show interest in the position and company, even if it is not your top choice.
3. *Eye contact.* Maintain eye contact with all interviewers throughout the interview.
4. *Examples.* Use specific examples of past employment and performance to answer the questions.

At Alltel, Lara Crain said she prefers candidates who exhibit an "ability to adapt and grow." Again, always accentuate the positive, even when the subject matter is dark and unsettling.

Some job interviews are grueling, some are push-up exercises for the uninitiated, some are hugely successful, but all job interviews are the moment you have been waiting for, so seize the opportunity and enjoy it—or at least be thankful that you have gotten this far. Remember all job interviews are uniquely challenging. If your last meeting with a prospective employer raised your stress level, take a look at "The Art of Interviewing," by Gregory Favre,[10] and read how Sandy Rowe, the editor of the *Portland Oregonian,* conducts a job interview.

In the interview, I'm trying to determine what I think of the person and his/her chance of success rather than focusing primarily on the specific journalistic skill. I want to get to know the candidate as a person—and sometimes I succeed pretty well. My competitive streak makes me want to find out things about the applicant that the eight or twelve others who talk to them don't find out. I frequently do. The first time I interviewed Jane Weaver for a job (I hired her twice) she left my office and reportedly told someone in the newsroom, "My God, that woman knows everything but my shoe size." That's my goal. I want to know what motivates applicants; what has been the greatest challenge or biggest disappointment they have faced (either personally or professionally) and how they dealt with it; what things make them angry or happy; what they are passionate about outside of family; what relationships are most important to them and always, always WHY. It is not unusual for an applicant (male or female) to cry in an interview because of some emotional chord I've touched. I try to lead an applicant to be introspective and from that to glean some idea of their values and their level of self-awareness, both of which are critical to success. My questions are open-ended and psychological enough that one applicant, mid-interview, moved from the chair where he was sitting to the sofa in my office, reclined on the sofa, looked at me and said, "Next question, doctor." I hired him.

6

THE INNER CIRCLE

*"I always ask open-ended questions so that it's rare
that I get a one-word or two-word answer."*

NEIL BUSSELL
Group Manager
PepsiCo Business Solutions Group

You are almost there. You made it past the gate-keeper in human resources and now you are about to be introduced to the people you will be working with—provided that you, once again, prove that you will be an asset to the company. Although many Fortune 500 respondents said they do not always immediately follow up one interview with another that same day, you should be prepared nonetheless to meet with more than one person after your initial face-to-face interview. That's one of the reasons why it's important you have several copies of your formatted résumé on hand.

In fact, at large companies you can expect to meet up to seven or eight people—depending, of course, on the level of the position. *All* of the Fortune 500 respondents agreed that when a company is interested in a candidate, more than one interview is conducted, so you can be certain that you will meet with more individuals after the initial face-to-face if the company is interested in hiring you.

It's hard to generalize how long the interview process takes because each company approaches it differently, and a number of other variables (such as rapport, level of position, etc.) must be factored into the equation. Assume that the more senior the position, the longer the interview. But generally, and according to 76 percent of the Fortune 500 respondents, an interview lasts about an hour. Remember, though, that you may be asked to proceed immediately to your next interview with a department head or for a technical interview. If that is the case, the interview process can last more than two hours—sometimes even a whole day (or in some cases maybe even two days). The HR representative gives you a rundown of how long the process normally takes, but don't be afraid to ask if this is not addressed.

The important thing to remember is that you should keep your interview day clear of other obligations. When you go on a job interview, your primary purpose is to get an offer, so you don't want to rush through this process because you have an important meeting or obligation later in the day. Take the day off from your other job if possible—or at the very least mention the time frame for which you are available prior to meeting for the face-to-face. You don't want to excuse yourself from an interview that is going extremely well because a prior commitment beckons.

TECHNICALLY SPEAKING

Many jobs today require that you exhibit technical proficiency. The company determines this proficiency by administering a test or a technical interview or even a technical presentation. Sometimes HR administers the test; sometimes you must go to the department in which you will work to test or give a technical interview. TIAA-CREF's generalist, Robert Moll, said his company rarely tests, but when a test is necessary for a specific job, then it is given in the human resources department "to ensure that it is consistently administered and tracked." The test may be given at your first face-to-face, but sometimes you must return to the site for another visit. Obviously, it varies from company to company and from one position to the next. What's important to remember is that you observe all interview formalities. If you are asked to return and take a test, make sure you are dressed appropriately—just as if you were meeting for the very first time. Every meeting with the future employer is critical, so don't assume you can approach it casually. Even though good technicians are highly valued in today's marketplace, the rituals still must be observed. The job interview is a formal process: from start to finish.

THE THINKING PROCESS

The technical interview gives the employer insight into how you think and how you process information. Unlike other phases of the interview—where interpersonal skills play a major role—the results of technical interviews or tests are quantifiable. Either you know your stuff or you don't.

But that doesn't mean you can't prepare for a technical interview or test. As with every other phase of the interview process, the more you know about the company or industry or field, the better prepared you are for the technical interview. For instance, at PSEG in Newark (the largest utility in New Jersey with more than 10,000 employees), the *PSEG Career Guide* is on the company's Web site.[1] The guide, which can be found on the Career Page, provides a sample test that the company gives to all entry-level applicants. This test ensures that employees have the basic knowledge necessary to perform their jobs well at this particular company. At BellSouth, "If you are being considered for a job within BellSouth, you will be informed of what selection screens are required for that job. Each screen has a study guide associated with it. Study guides describe the selection screen and provide information (TIPs) that may help candidates perform well."[2] Knowing ahead of time what to expect on the test will make the entire interview go more smoothly. How?

For one, you will not be caught off guard. You want to come across as the ultimate professional during your job interview. If you get rattled when the HR representative leads you to an empty office and hands you the test, you are not creating the best impression. Professionals know how to manage expectations in a calm and confident manner. Second, these tests occasionally require you to use skills that may be a bit rusty (geometry, for example). Third, the turmoil of not being prepared can wreak havoc on your demeanor for the rest of the interview. That's why it's so important to know what's expected and brush up ahead of time. Usually you are given advance notice on a test requirement and you have a chance to prepare, but occasionally there is no notice. Try to find out what the expectations are in your field or at that particular company ahead of time. In a very competitive job market, this type of preparation gives you an edge.

Other professions may require even more grueling testing—the kind of testing that puts your expertise on the line and makes you sweat. Technical interviews at Microsoft are notorious for stumping programmers.[3] Microsoft's tech interview supposedly is crammed with tons of tricky questions regarding data structures, algorithms, and logic puzzles. In fact, some techies actually sell information on the Web about their failed attempts at Microsoft interviews. Obviously, the tech interview at Microsoft is top secret, but, again, it still pays to review as much as possible. You might want to take a look at a book considered the "bible" for programmers: *Programming Interviews Exposed,* by John Mongan and Noah Suojanen.[4] Another useful book—regardless of whether your tech interview is at Microsoft or at XYZ—is William Poundstone's *How Would You Move Mount Fuji?*

Even seemingly nontechnical industries have test requirements as well. At newspapers and magazines, for instance, copy editors must test during a job inerview. One way to review for that test is by taking a look at the 50-page "Editing Booklet"[6] on http://www.copydesk.org (as well as by reviewing applicable stylebooks, such as the 15th edition of *The Chicago Manual of Style,* University of Chicago Press, 2003, and the most recent edition of *The Associated Press Stylebook*). Bill Walsh, author and founder of TheSlot.com,[7] advises copy editors to "memorize the AP stylebook and a good list of the most commonly misspelled words, and you'll out-test 90-something percent of the competition, no matter how much experience they have. If you can test well *and* interview well, you're in."

At the corporate communications department at Verizon, Peter Thonis, senior vice president of external communications, said some applicants are given an hour or two to write a sample press release. Thonis said, "We want them to do a press release just to make sure they can do it. And you can tell a lot by just the way someone writes a press release what kind of writer he or she is." Thonis said he prefers this type of testing to relying solely on the candidate's writing samples because he is primarily interested in seeing how well and how fast the candidate can write. He explained, "Sampling is an interesting thing because very often in this business whatever you have written has already been edited. So I really don't know how good a writer you are. What I'm looking for is somebody who is a good writer but, even more important, a good writer who is fast. When I look at samples, I don't know whether it took the person ten minutes or 15 days. What I really want is someone who can write something quickly."

Do your research (was that already mentioned?) before the interview. Find out what is required, and study if you can. Remember that analogy of a job interview being similar to an open-book test? The comparison is true.

MOVING UPSTAIRS

Once you have discussed your qualifications and skill set with the initial interviewer, the focus begins to shift slightly from you to the prospective job and company. Neil Bussell, a group manager with the PepsiCo Business Solutions Group, maintains that by the time he meets with a candidate, he has already prepared for the interview by reviewing the candidate's résumé. He trusts that the screening process has narrowed the pool of candidates to those who are specifically qualified to perform the job based on their skills and prior experience.

As noted earlier, you can usually expect some soft talk to open the interview. Bussell said, "The first thing I do is make the applicant comfortable in the setting. I generally do small talk to start." Even though the purpose of this soft introduction is to make you feel at ease, try to keep your own comments pleasant and positive (or at least neutral). Your interpersonal skills are being evaluated at every encounter in the interview process, so don't assume that an exchange about the weather cannot be a loaded topic of conversation if you are griping about the snow. At all times during the interview process, you want to give the impression that you are an easy person to be around—and that spending eight hours or more in your company will not be an endurance test.

Remember that a job interview is not just *all about you*. Expect to get a detailed briefing about what the company does and what the specific job entails, especially if the business is esoteric and difficult to assess from initial research. The interviewer wants to make sure that the candidate is comfortable with the nature of the business or can make the necessary adjustments if the type of business is new or a stretch. Your comfort level is important and you can expect questions that will ascertain whether you can fit into the job, the department, and the organization.

Once you progress to the second interview, interviewers are often trying to assess whether you have the right chemistry to work in the department. Another layer, however, of questioning may be directed at your level of interest in the job and the company. As you have already met with human resources, you have picked up some information along the way. Don't ignore what you have learned. You want to exhibit a level of interest that suggests you have paid attention to the information that was given to you by the human resources professional. By the time you get past the gatekeeper, the department head or second interviewer expects that you have some grounding in the business (besides what you discovered in your own research). Provided you like what you see at this stage, it is a good idea to begin to sell your interest in the company.

Bussell said that when he meets with candidates, his primary purpose is to "review their experiences with them and their roles on [former] projects." Your responses should show that you are a solutions-oriented, can-do individual—someone who is able to offer verifiable results and specific instances where you achieved your goals. You should be able to highlight your career accomplishments without appearing arrogant or brash, which is always a fine line.

At this point, Bussell likes to ask candidates, "What would your manager tell me about you?" It's his favorite question because "it's great to hear what people say or how they think they are perceived. Then I ask the same question about their business partners or internal clients or external vendors. If the role happens to be someone who is going to manage a vendor: 'What would the vendor most often say about you?'" Make sure all of these topics have been given some thought, but don't sound as though you are repeating a memorized script. Bussell thought a good answer to these questions "indicates the candidate's ability to think on his or her feet."

As preparation for this stage of the interview process, you might want to review your work history with the following topics in mind, topics that appeared originally in *Get the Interview Every Time:*[8]

- Your past relationships with your boss and coworkers
- Your respect for the values of others
- Your ability to meet deadlines in a timely fashion
- Your ability to rally support for a project
- Your value-oriented approach to problem solving
- Your efficient use of time
- Your ability to multitask, especially in cross-functional aspects of a project
- Your initiative
- Your ability to address all the small details but always keeping your focus on the bigger picture
- Your commitment to continual learning
- Your thorough knowledge of the industry
- Your ability to adapt to your surroundings as well as to the personalities of those with whom you work
- Your ability to remove obstacles

After the introductory small talk, focus on the job you did and the job you want to do. Don't be tempted to go off on a tangent—unless you are specifically asked to speak about your extracurricular activities or interests. Also, do not be overly preoccupied with what you said or what you are going to say next. Stay in the moment. Besides, it's unlikely that one wrong answer will disqualify you. Bussell said, "I try not to make any snap judgments as I am going through. It's very rare that I would end an interview early based on an answer or even a series of answers, although I have done that once or twice. The vast majority of time I give them the benefit of the interview."

This has been stressed again and again: employers value employees with strong interpersonal skills, and a great deal depends on your ability to communicate effectively. This ability has a direct impact on how well you work within the team as well as in your dealings with senior executives. But if your strength lies more in the realm of knowledge than with people, don't immediately count yourself out of the running.

According to Bussell: "I don't judge a technician solely on his or her communication skills, because good technicians are as hard to find as good communicators. There has to be a certain level of communication; the person has to have a minimum of social graces. For instance, not doing inappropriate things at an interview, certainly not using foul language, but basically there has to be a culture fit. If the person is a little bit shy, that's not going to be a negative. I came up through the technical rank, and I can still talk enough tech to make the person feel comfortable in an interview."

So if you are not a "great communicator," but you are a good technician, what are some of the basic social graces?

- Make eye contact.
- Maintain appropriate behavior (remain formal and professional, even if the interviewer has his feet on the desk while quizzing you).
- Pay attention.
- Exhibit interest in the job.
- Respect the interviewer's time.
- Ask relevant questions.
- Provide thoughtful answers.

These are the minimum expectations at an interview, whether you are introverted or not. To alleviate self-consciousness, be interested instead of interesting, which allows you to zero in on the specifics of the job, the department, and the company.

NOW IT'S YOUR TURN

If you have made it this far, count on the interviewer to do some selling as well. The interviewer already knows you are qualified, so a lot of what transpires at this point revolves around what the company has to offer you, such as the type of work environment, the kinds of projects you will be involved with, the type of people you will be reporting to or managing, or the type of culture the company projects. You are free to ask as many questions as you see fit, but, according to Sherri Martin of Deere, "The interviewee should not take over the discussion with too many questions." Art Calderon, a director of human resources and strategic programs for Phelps Dodge Corporation, added that "the candidate should always be respectful of the interviewer's time and schedule."

Keep the 50-50 ratio in mind at all times during the interview process and remember that when it comes to interpersonal skills, listening is just as integral as talking. Again, read the signals and don't ask 100 questions if you sense that the interviewer is trying to wrap things up.

Bussell said he never gets impatient with questions, which "means the candidate is interested and engaged. It's great answering questions. It shows the person listens, especially when he or she can connect to what I said and then ask further questions."

A PLURALITY VOTE

The panel interview can be intimidating: three, four, five people sitting at a table looking you up and down and even inside out. Not only do you have to make eye contact, but now you have to make eye contact with everyone in the room without favoring one person over another. That's the easy part because essentially what's being evaluated in a panel interview is your skill with groups—or how well you interact with individuals in a group setting.

On many levels, a panel interview makes perfect sense. A business environment is a group environment. No one works in isolation. As an employee, you'll be expected to deal with key players in various organizational units on a daily basis, so your interpersonal skills are of primary concern to a prospective employer. How well you know how to build relationships at the new company is a key to your success there.

You may be outnumbered in a panel interview, but the good news is that a panel interview can work to your advantage as well. Think about it. Instead of meeting with three, four, five people throughout the day (which can be draining), you meet with the panel. Ideally, the panel gives you an opportunity to meet with several representatives of varying levels at the company. It is likely that every member of the panel provides a different point of view or reference regarding the company, so the information you receive tends to be more balanced and thorough. Rest assured that a serious comparison of notes transpires after the interview, but at least the panel is evaluating you while you are at your best and not at the end of a grueling day of three, four, five individual interviews.

Every organization and company handles the panel interview differently. Sometimes the panels are small (three or four people); sometimes they are large (seven or eight). Just remember that the real challenge will be in building a rapport with the various interviewers. Try with every ounce of egalitarian goodwill in you to make a connection with every member on the panel—at least on some level.

At Verizon, a company of 210,000 employees, panel interviews are not unusual. Verizon's Thonis said his company is a "very flat organization," which means there are not a lot of layers of bureaucracy between the applicant and the job. Thonis tells a representative from human resources that he needs someone to fill a certain position and then he puts out feelers to find that person. "HR is involved in the sense it knows about our need, but that department doesn't contact the applicant. We contact the person. We would never hire someone inexperienced, so we usually find them by virtue of somebody in the business who knows of somebody who is looking. That person says to us, 'You know, you should really look at this person' or 'I know this person is interviewing,' and then we go after him or her. There is no HR at this point," Thonis said.

In a recent panel interview, Thonis said three members of his department interviewed three candidates for an open position. By the time the applicants showed up for the interview, the panel had already determined that all three were qualified for the position. "First of all, I know from the résumé whether he or she is a viable candidate," Thonis said.

Although Verizon is a massive company, Thonis said the corporate communications department recruits talent like a "very small, high-level, intimate shop." But the senior vice president of external communications said there is nothing intimidating about a panel interview in his department. Most recently, three people—the person the candidate is going to work for, his boss, and Thonis—composed the panel. "We basically don't sit there and conspire on the questions. We really have a conversation." In fact, he said the atmosphere is relaxed, and he gets the candidates to open up by "engaging them in war stories."

The people who compose the panel already understand what skills are necessary to perform the job. In fact, the members of the panel are all on the same page as to what it takes to succeed in the corporate communications department at Verizon. What Thonis tries to gauge is whether candidates possess the necessary traits for the particular job. Many Fortune 500 respondents said the same thing. They try to discover if a candidate has certain personal qualities that are not only integral to performing the job but also display the person's ability to get along with others in that particular corporate culture.

"I am looking for some very specific traits, and those traits I'm going to find out in the conversation. I'm not going to find them out by grilling them about what they know about the business. I want to make sure they are intelligent because they are not going to be experts in telecom, especially if they come to us from outside the business. But I do expect them to know what they are doing in terms of media relations."

Because most of the candidates Verizon hires for this department have solid reputations in the business and are not unknown commodities; the panel can jump right in and start to delve and dig. Don't forget that the underlying question running through every hiring manager's mind during a job interview is, "Can I work well with this person?"

To get the conversation going, Thonis said he asks questions such as, "I hear you worked in XYZ's office. What's the most fun you've had? What's the most stressful thing you've done? What are you most proud of?" Thonis said he keeps the dialogue as informal as possible, "so that people are just acting naturally." This reinforces another theme in the Fortune 500 surveys. Again and again, hiring professionals advised job seekers to be themselves. In other words, the job interview should not be an Oscar-winning performance. You may win an offer with a performance, but your chances of making a good match are minimal. Find a position that suits who you are—as far as skills, experience, *and* personality go.

Thonis looks for particular personal traits when evaluating candidates. He responded that "first, they have to be strong writers." Although Thonis is interviewing candidates for corporate communications, communication skills topped the list of most Fortune 500 respondents—whether the department was marketing or finance. "You're really trying to look for verbal and communication skills," Thonis said. "Strong writers may sound like a no-brainer, but there are many communication teams around the country where most of the people are not strong writers. They might be better than average writers, but they are not strong writers."

MAKING THE CONNECTION

Throughout the book emphasis has been placed on building a rapport with the interviewer. In many respects, rapport has a lot to do with *fit*—how well you fit the position, how well you fit into the corporate culture, and how well you fit into the department. The interviewer can actually visualize you in the new position because in many respects you share many of the same ideas and values. Engelhard's Mangiarano drove home this point and so did Thonis.

Hiring managers basically hire people very much like themselves. Rapport goes beyond skin color or race or gender, even though corporations are eager to have diverse employees who reflect the general population. Rapport has more to do with what's going on inside, regardless of what your outside looks like. Hiring managers want to know what drives the candidate. If it's the same as what drives them—energy, ambition, initiative, team orientation—then there's a fairly good chance they will recognize those characteristics in you and bring you on board. On some level, for a good match to be made they have to connect with you and you have to connect with them.

Tight deadlines and breaking stories are commonplace in Verizon's communications department. The atmosphere is intense at this "shop," so the second characteristic Thonis looks for in a candidate is the ability to produce very good writing in a pressure-cooker environment. He makes the distinction between managing pressure and loving pressure: "People who *thrive* under pressure, not people who do well under pressure. There's a difference. There are people who do well under pressure but don't like it, and they will burn out. We like our people to love pressure. They take anxiety and channel it into productive energy. And that's the way I am. The more pressure I'm under, the better I do. And those are the kind of people I like."

Preparation is key to a successful interview, but you have to face it, some jobs just aren't suitable—no matter how much you think you can transform yourself. It goes back to what Sherri Martin of Deere said: "Realize that not every position you interview for will be the right job for you." That's why it's essential that you recognize what makes you tick—what brings you satisfaction, what gets your adrenaline going, what matters to you most in the workplace. That type of research you cannot do on the Web.

Thonis knows his own strengths and looks for the same qualities when building his team of communicators at Verizon: "If you look at me, for example, I'm a good writer. I am a very good fast writer, so if you say to me I need a five-page paper and I need it in one hour flat, I can write it and it will be good. Will it be excellent? It will be *good*. Somebody would say, 'Oh my God, if you had five hours to write it, it would be excellent.' It probably wouldn't be any better. I'm really good really fast, but I'm not necessarily better if you give me more time."

When hiring managers evaluate candidates, they are asking themselves: "Do these candidates work like me? Do they value teamwork? Do they burn the midnight oil? Are they can-do people who know how to finish strongly?" That's what the face-to-face is all about, and that's why it's so important that you pick yourself up and brush yourself off when you don't get the offer. You won't be happy if you work at a job or in an environment that doesn't challenge you, and you won't last long if you feel like an outsider in an atmosphere where everyone works weekends, and you are constantly longing for regular bouts of salmon fishing at a mountain stream.

Ask yourself, "Where do I work best?" "What brings out my strong points?" and then honor it—no matter what type of work it is. Recognize that this is what you are good at, and then always be ready to stretch yourself too. So be good at what you do . . . and grow. Success will come.

RELATIONSHIP BUILDING

Chapter 7 goes into more detail about the personal qualities that are valued by Fortune 500 hiring managers—the attributes that help you build the kind of relationships you need to thrive in your industry—but Thonis also touched on this topic when he described the third characteristic he looks for in a candidate for his department.

He said he wants someone who knows how to navigate in the workplace by building strong relationships. "And the third [characteristic] is being able to work through and with people. It's about relationship building. And it's about trust and integrity. And it's about the ability to get things done through other people.

Because we are a very, very big business here with 210,000 employees, and no one person has all the information. So you have to be able to work with people," Thonis explained.

Whether you intend to work at a large organization or a small start-up, however, word spreads. Newcomers to the job market sometimes assume that the world is bigger than it really is. It may feel at times like a cold and anonymous world, but industries are much smaller than they at first appear. You build a reputation at every job—and that reputation precedes you to the next level. Decide from the get-go to do your best, follow protocol, and not burn bridges (even if you believe your former boss could use a little shock therapy).

Thonis continued: "They have to trust you enough to know that what you are doing is important enough to be able to drag them out of meetings at a moment's notice and have the person not say, 'I'll get back to you.'" This is a common thread throughout the surveys. John Garofalo, an enterprise staffing and outreach manager at PSEG, said, "We do assess candidates on job-related competencies relevant to the position. For example, a manager would be assessed through a behavioral-style interview on his or her honesty and integrity, building credibility and trust, accountability, decisive action taking, and emotional intelligence." Hiring managers need the face-to-face interview—either a panel or one-on-one meeting—to determine whether candidates possess these attributes. A résumé, after all, cannot do justice to this side of the candidate.

ARRIVING AT A DECISION

For those still dreading the thought of a panel interview, another advantage is that a consensus is arrived at more quickly than if the candidate went on five individual interviews. The comparison of notes often takes place immediately after the interview. Thonis said, "Usually, especially if the candidate is a person we happen to know, we make a decision right away. The last time, we [the panel] talked about it for 15 minutes, and we all agreed on the person. We moved."

The panel interview can cut the process by half through eliminating several days of interviewing or, in some circumstances, several hours of interviewing. When a cross section of staff is on the panel, the results of the interview are even more objective. Add to this the fact that members of the panel tend to put their best feet forward when they are among their peers, and you have a winning combination—as long as you can get over your initial discomfort.

7

WHAT FORTUNE 500 EMPLOYERS VALUE

"We have seven guiding values at our company: respect for people; speed, simplicity, and agility; relentless pursuit of quality; communication; customer focus; innovation; accountability."

BILL VLCEK
Manager of Strategic Staffing
International Truck & Engine Company

In the survey, Fortune 500 hiring professionals were asked what they value in an employee. Initially, it was surprising to see that honesty, integrity, and trust led the way (with communication skills next in line). Most likely companies have been influenced by the fact that the business world has been turned upside down by recent events—cooked books, outlandish CEO perks, insider trading, to name some of the allegations directed at isolated companies—so guiding values have been pushed to the forefront.

But as so many Fortune 500 respondents emphasized, a company's success essentially depends on the quality of its business relationships. Because honesty, integrity, and trust are integral to good relationships, employees who share these values fortify the core of the company. Great employees, great company: it's that simple. So putting the best people in the job has become a hallowed quest for corporations. Some companies learned this lesson the hard way, whereas other companies always maintained high standards, but all companies today are highly sensitive to "the company they keep." A lot is lost when a corporate image is tarnished.

Corporate image and business relationships are key issues in hiring. That is for certain, but an even bigger quandary is the near impossibility of turning an unproductive, complaining employee into a positive, can-do contributor—no matter how motivating the executive team—without a lot of effort, which would be better spent on growing the business. Expectations at companies, then, are that employees bring these strengths to the workplace.

When describing Nucor's primary strength in *Good to Great*,[1] Jim Collins had this to say: "In determining 'the right people,' the good-to-great companies placed greater weight on character attributes than on specific educational background, practical skills, specialized knowledge, or work experience. Not that specific knowledge or skills are unimportant, but they viewed these traits as more teachable (or at least learnable), whereas they believed dimensions like character, work ethic, basic intelligence, dedication to fulfilling commitments, and values are more ingrained."

As a result, values and personal attributes have been nudged into the limelight and now job seekers are expected to examine how those very same values function in their work life. Engelhard's Mangiarano contended that "we all share a fairly common set of values, and we ensure everyone is highly ethical." Rather than relying solely on references to attest to applicants' good character, in an interview Mangiarano asks probing questions that compel these applicants to think long and hard about the variables of ethical behavior in the workplace. "Work-disrupting character flaws," as Richard Bolles referred to them, are often discovered as a result of this line of questioning.[2]

Even though most job candidates are prepared to address their strong organizational skills or problem-solving abilities or initiative at a job interview, questions that delve into their character can throw them, because applicants generally don't consider how integrity or trust or accountability has impacted their job performance. Host Marriott's Whittington will say to an applicant, "Tell me what you value," and Phelps Dodge's Calderon said candidates stumble when he says, "Describe what safety means to you as a personal value." From the Fortune 500 responses, these types of questions need to be considered when you examine your work history in preparation for a job interview. Know what core values motivate you, and then plan to talk about them in detail if you are asked.

According to Lamoureux of Energy East, "We tend to use a lot of the behavioral interviewing questions, so it would probably be those types of behavior-oriented questions, such as 'Tell me about a time you . . .' or 'Give me an example . . .' that people stumble over most often. Candidates typically need more time to think before they respond to these types of questions. They are hard questions to answer, so the candidate should take his or her time."

On the flip side, knowing ahead of time what an employer values makes your job search more successful—as well as providing you with the job satisfaction you deserve. In an article, "Employee Satisfaction Slacks Off After Time on the Job,"[3] Anita Bruzzese said this: "According to recently published research, there is a 'significant decline in employees' overall job satisfaction after they've been working for their employer for six months or more, and overall job satisfaction continues to decline the longer a worker puts in time for an employer."

What happens? Initially, employees are enthusiastic about their prospects at a company, but then "broken equipment," "endless meetings," and self-centered managers who focus on those employees "allergic to work" instead of focusing on the group set the tone. When you interview for a job, then, a company's core values should be as important to you as your good character is to them. Try to discover what the company values before you accept a job offer. Ask your own probing questions.

In *Maximum Success,* the authors wrote: "No one is going to define the culture for you . . . the burden is on you to carefully observe and gather data about the culture that you will live in day in and day out should you accept the job."[4]

PERSONAL QUALITIES

The Fortune 500 hiring professionals were asked to list the most important personal qualities in a job candidate. With integrity and communications skills leading the way, a number of other qualities were also cited. Take a look at the attributes described in the following sections that Fortune 500 employers value. You may want to consider how they pertain to your own work history and how you can best address these personal qualities at your job interview.

Then consider the questions that follow each personal quality. No one has all of these personal qualities, but everyone has a few of them. Try to see how these qualities relate to the workplace as well as to your work history. Find the right words to describe your strengths. The better able you are to answer these questions—and even provide examples of how you demonstrated these qualities at work—the more prepared you will be for your interview. Remember to be specific with examples of how you demonstrated these qualities when you answer the questions.

Integrity, Honesty, Sincerity, and Trust

Employees who exhibit these characteristics are good for their word. When they are asked to produce, they deliver. When they are asked to show up, they are on time. They share their expertise and are able to honor and respect others. They tell the truth. They act as a resource for less experienced workers. They maintain company standards. They honor their commitments inside and outside the office. They do not dabble in falsehoods. They are direct and precise, even when a position may be unpopular. They are credible so that trust can be established. They take responsibility for their actions and refrain from pointing fingers.

- Did you meet your deadlines?
- Are projects completed in a timely fashion?
- Do you have good relationships with your coworkers, peers, and supervisor?
- Do you put a high value on honesty and sincerity?
- Do you share your knowledge of systems and processes?
- Are you helpful to less experienced coworkers?
- Are you straightforward with your boss, peers, and subordinates?
- Do you inspire confidence?
- Are you trustworthy?
- Do you deliver what you promise?
- Are you included in confidential discussions on matters pertaining to the business?
- How do you tap into the diversity of your colleagues?
- Do you listen attentively at meetings to all members of the group?
- Do you observe the boundaries or personal space of others with whom you work?
- Are you reliable?
- Do you put your team or group before yourself?
- Are you considerate of the need for quiet?
- Are you sensitive to the tight schedules of your coworkers?

Communication Skills

Employees with strong communication skills listen actively and respond clearly. They are direct and to the point. Their e-mails are clear and concise. They don't hedge, fudge, or misconstrue information. They can be counted on to explain complex processes simply. They choose their words carefully. They are committed to improving their speaking, listening, and writing skills. They appreciate the facts.

- Do you listen attentively to everyone—whether it's the assistant in the mailroom or the CEO?
- Do you cut away the superfluous and zero in on the important facts in all your communication?
- Do you pride yourself on speaking and writing clearly?
- Are you committed to continual learning regarding your communication skills?
- Do you choose your words carefully—across all mediums—even in e-mail?

- Do you communicate face-to-face whenever possible, or do you hide behind technology, such as e-mail, voice mail, or text messaging?
- Do you respect others' time and keep your communication brief and to the point?
- Can you describe complexities with simplicity?
- Do you look people in the eye when you speak?
- Do you refrain from belittling conversations?
- Do you ask questions before you act?
- Do you provide deliberate and thoughtful answers full of specifics—whether you are writing an e-mail, speaking to your supervisor, or composing a memo directed at your business unit?

Customer Service Oriented

Employees who are customer focused know that the "customer is the real boss," according to Jeffrey Fox in *How to Become a Great Boss.* Their priority is to remove obstacles and provide timely service no matter what. They are dedicated to expanding the customer base in order to grow the business. They know that good numbers on the bottom line depend on customer satisfaction—no matter what the business is. They can readily define who the customer is. In fact, they know the customer inside out and upside down. Their primary purpose is to provide good service and keep customers happy.

- Do you have a positive and helpful manner toward customers?
- Do you return all phone calls?
- Do you cut through red tape to deliver results?
- Do you put the customer before yourself?
- Do you know that your job depends on satisfied customers?
- Are you able to follow through, even when a customer is dissatisfied?
- Can you turn a bad situation into a good one by resolving all matters as quickly as possible so that the customer returns?
- Do you maintain relationships with customers who are not currently active?
- Do you value customers' feedback?

Dedication and Loyalty

Employees who are dedicated and loyal invest themselves in their jobs, careers, and companies. They show up consistently and are motivated to perform to the best of their ability. They are positive about the company, their coworkers and their supervisors. They are engaged by their work and not sidetracked by the next opportunity. They are committed for an extended period. They follow direction and provide support for the company's goals and objectives. They manage the way they would like to be managed. They report for duty ungrudgingly.

- Do you see a job through—even when the course gets bumpy?
- Do you believe in the company's products and/or services?
- Are you engaged by your daily responsibilities?
- Do you take direction or constructive criticism without becoming defensive?
- Can you have a heated discussion and then come to a consensus, even if your ideas were rejected?
- Are you open to change?
- Can you change course with the company?
- Can you perform effectively *all* the responsibilities of your job?
- Do you show up on time and ready for a full days' work?
- Do you pride yourself on your work habits?

Positive, Friendly, Can-Do Personality

Employees who are positive and friendly maintain good relationships with their coworkers, peers, supervisors, customers, and clients. They have a can-do attitude, regardless of the scope or difficulties of a project. They are pleasant to be around and remain professional under all circumstances. They refrain from complaining and negative comments. They are not easily overwhelmed or continually stressed. They have a sense of humor, especially when the going gets tough. They seek the solution instead of being mired in the problem.

- Are you engaged by your work?
- Do you smile often?
- Are you helpful and agreeable?
- Do you validate others?
- Do you seek answers to problems instead of being a problem?
- Do you approach difficulties with quick resolutions in mind?
- Do you encourage others to do their best?
- Do you provide service happily and without resentment?
- Do you tackle difficult projects with enthusiasm?
- Do you provide others with opportunities to grow?
- Are you someone others like to be around?

Strong Work Ethic

Employees with a strong work ethic routinely perform above and beyond what is required. They are committed to their job and their organization. They are willing to work long hours when necessary and are available whenever a crisis arises—at any time of day or night. They take pride in their output and seek ways to ensure continuous improvement. They do not shirk responsibilities. They are self-motivated. They articulate objectives clearly so that others can embrace them. They continually sharpen their knowledge so that they become an expert resource for their peers as well as the company.

- Do you make yourself available to others?
- Are you willing to work extra hours to meet a deadline or correct a problem?
- Do you routinely improve efficiency and procedures?
- Do you act as an expert resource to others?
- Do you manage priorities well?
- Do you work out contingency plans when a work path is blocked?
- Are you passionate about your work?
- Do you gain momentum or lose steam on most projects?
- Do you commit yourself fully to the task or project at hand?
- Are you able to identify potential problems before they arise?
- Are you fulfilled when a job is completed and done well?

Teamwork Oriented

Employees who value the team above individual effort know that good results depend on a lot of support. They put a high priority on healthy working relationships. They are willing to share the credit. They know that opposing ideas can spur better ideas. They recognize that others play a significant role in their success. They reward and validate those who support the group. They are friendly toward big ideas, new people, changed courses, and better plans because they have support and cooperation from their peers. They know how to work well with others.

- Do you set reasonable deadlines?
- Are you cooperative?
- Do you value the input of others?
- Do you trust that your coworkers can do as good a job as you can?
- Do you share in the decision-making process?

- Do you delegate comfortably?
- Do you take pride in joint efforts?
- Do you share the limelight?
- Do you teach or coach every day?
- Are you happy to see your coworkers?
- Are you attracted to collaborative projects?
- Do you remain enthusiastic until a project is completed?
- Do you share your coworkers' values while being respectful of their differences?
- Is your door open to everyone in your group?
- Are you able to identify your role in a group and play it even if it is not the star-player position?
- Are you more interested in contributing than leading?
- Do you recognize other people's strengths or accommodate when necessary?
- Do you do your part so others can do theirs?
- Do you build a consensus before you act?

Initiative

Employees who display initiative do what needs to be done without being reminded. They are driven by curiosity. They are often fearless. They consider mistakes learning tools. They fall in love with ideas and then figure out a way to make those ideas concrete. They act without being nudged. They are self-motivated. They are often independent thinkers. Sometimes they are bold. They are usually creative. They are sure of themselves. They feel comfortable leading others. They like to investigate further.

- Are you confident of your abilities?
- Will you follow an idea to its logical conclusion?
- Do you prefer acting independently?
- Are you continually seeking creative solutions to confounding problems?
- Do you like to be challenged?
- Do you sign up for projects?
- Do you tackle problems no one else touches?
- Are you eager to try new methods, processes, or strategies?
- Do you persist until you find a solution?
- Do you dislike being micromanaged?
- Do you tread where others dare not go?
- Are you confident when going it alone?

Strong Organizational Skills

Employees who have strong organizational skills know how to pull all the pieces together so that a coherent and logical conclusion—of the project or the filing system or the systems integration—is reached. They can transform scattered or unrelated matter—whether it is information, ingredients, hardware, data, or engine parts—into a finished product. Order appeals to their finer sense. Logic lifts their spirit. They are advocates of flow charts, chains of command, graphs and tables, PowerPoint, and color-coded filing systems. They know how to make sense out of confusion and chaos. They quantify results.

- Are you logical?
- Are you quick in identifying patterns?
- Do you equate a neat desk with a clear-thinking mind?
- Are you most comfortable when all the details fall in line?
- Do you prioritize quickly?
- Do you impose order on whatever is thrown at you?
- Will you throw away the superfluous to maintain reason?
- Will you bend over backward to make things right again?
- Do you perform corrective actions regularly?
- Are you always looking for new time-management strategies?
- Do you highlight key issues in multiple, cross-functional projects?
- Do you act as an integration resource for other staff?
- Are you eager to straighten things out all the time?
- Do you place a high value on efficiency?
- Do you pay attention to or keep track of every detail?

Speed, Simplicity, and Agility

Employees who exhibit these traits have a deep appreciation for the better mousetrap. They like things that work well. They believe in simple designs. They streamline. They don't waste people's time. They don't waste their own time. They are inventive. They provide simple directions for complex mechanisms. They believe in flow. If it's broken, they fix it and improve it. In all things, style must serve substance. They make difficult things look easy. They have little patience for bureaucracy and red tape. They get things done faster.

- Are you able to zero in on the problem and fix it quickly?
- Do you cherish good design?

- Are you an advocate of simplicity?
- Do you work till it works?
- Do you insist on improving quality control measures?
- Do you implement best practices?
- Are you constantly thinking about future contingencies and scalability?
- Do you recognize solutions and take action?
- Do you manage integration well?
- Do you engage in planning, design, and optimization?
- Are you committed to timely resolutions?
- Do you respond to problems in an efficient manner?
- Do you test until it's perfect?
- Can you spot a malfunction a mile away?
- Are you an advocate of standards?
- Do you continually improve products and services?

Decision-Making Ability

Employees capable of making sound, judicious, and fiscally responsible decisions based on knowledge and expertise are highly prized. They recognize an opportunity and then act. They take responsibility for good and bad choices. They recognize the status quo but continually raise the bar. They are not afraid of new directions, remaining flexible at all times. They are confident of their expertise. They drive change and innovation. The right decisions seem obvious, even if they are unpopular. They process and prioritize information. They define elements and conditions to be resolved and then act. They understand dynamics and are sensitive to all key constituencies. They consider all the facts. They ask a lot of questions.

- Are you thoughtful or impulsive?
- Are you capable of seeing different points of view?
- Do you have a good sense of direction?
- Do you engage in intense internal debate?
- Are you responsive to others' needs and concerns?
- Do you consider all options before you act?
- How do you react when none of the options is acceptable?
- Do you conceptualize and implement broad-based strategies?
- Are you patient with complexity?
- Does ambiguity baffle you?
- Are you judicious?

- Do you ask a lot of questions?
- Do you leverage knowledge well?
- Do hard decisions make you uncomfortable?
- Do you factor in the human element?
- Do you consider the whole instead of just a particular part?
- Do you adapt well to change?

Respect for People

Employees who respect people are flexible and tolerant. They refrain from gossip and backbiting. They appreciate diversity. They are comfortable with different points of view. No matter how stressful the situation, they remain calm and judicious. They do not look for scapegoats or point fingers. They listen to opposing opinions. They refrain from stereotyping people. They care about the workplace community.

- Do you treat all employees with respect, regardless of their position?
- Do you demonstrate the appropriate reaction in your interactions with others?
- Do your cost-cutting measures affect your own pocketbook?
- Do you share information?
- Do you keep communication channels open and progress step-by-step?
- Do you listen to all ideas?
- Does diversity pique your interest?
- Are you supportive of coworkers?
- Do you strive to build teams?
- Do you maintain your composure even when the sky is falling?
- Do you recognize talent and reward it?
- Do you play by the rules?
- Are you comfortable with differences?
- Do you recognize potential in others?
- Do you communicate clearly what the best path is to achieve objectives?
- Do you give all employees and coworkers a chance to prove themselves?

Drive, Energy, Ambition

Employees who have drive, energy, and ambition are engaged by their work and continually seek ways to enhance their output. They are eager to get started.

They do not procrastinate. They believe in themselves. They develop strategies to achieve their goals. They are persistent and enthusiastic. They see roadblocks as challenges. They think about work when they are away from work. They are constructive and continually seek ways to build the business. They are disciplined and self-motivated.

- Do you look for ways to boost profitability?
- Are you committed to sustained growth?
- Do you take calculated risks?
- Do you have an exceptional track record based on quantifiable results?
- Do you consistently remove obstacles from the work path of others?
- Do you delegate judiciously?
- Are you highly productive?
- Are you able to prioritize in high-pressure situations?
- Do you have an affinity for breakthroughs?
- Can you let go of a losing enterprise without a serious deflation to your own ego or battering your coworkers?
- Are you still going strong after everyone else has tuckered out?
- Are you passionate about your work?

Problem-Solving Ability

Employees who solve problems consider all the facts—both good and bad—and seek solutions based on their expertise, familiarity with best practices, and in-depth knowledge of emerging trends or technology. They take necessary action instead of wishing problems would disappear. They confront hard realities—whether time constraints, production problems, budget restrictions, malfunctioning technology—and see options instead of impasses. They believe they can have an impact on a positive outcome. They prefer long-term solutions to short-term fixes. They favor step-by-step progress to stopgap measures. They are challenged rather than defeated by difficulty. The problem is less important than the solution.

- Do you optimize results for the short and long term?
- Do you consider all the variables and then act accordingly?
- Do you define plans by putting them through a rigorous process before committing to an action?
- Do you manage shifting priorities well?
- Do you articulate your objectives to those involved?

- Are you engaged when you detect patterns, develop projects, research options, interpret figures, or prove theories in an effort to discover a workable solution?
- Do you seek opportunities for revenue enhancement?
- Do you seek creative ways to cut costs without cutting key personnel?
- Do you look for answers in the not-so-obvious places?
- Are you curious about finding better ways to do things?
- Do you strive to be efficient?
- Are you always looking for better ways to accomplish goals?

Focus

Employees who are focused are capable of shutting out distractions and zeroing in on the problem or project at hand. They are not easily sidetracked. They utilize methodologies and strategies to achieve their aims. They move from point to point without losing momentum. They have faith that by looking hard at something, they will eventually find what they are looking for—even if they don't like what they see. They are engaged by their work. They clear away the superfluous to target the essential. They rarely procrastinate, but they also know that answers come during quiet intervals. Whether they are using their hands or their mind, they are fully present in the moment. They direct their energy at priorities.

- Do you shut out distractions to achieve your purpose?
- Are you committed to achieving the best results?
- Are you self-disciplined?
- Do you practice self-directed learning and critical evaluation?
- Do you actively promote the sharing of ideas?
- Do you change work behavior when greater efficiency or productivity measures are discovered?
- Do you actively monitor your own work, striving to continually improve your methods and strategies?
- Are you able to work conscientiously when a stressful environment sidetracks others?
- Are you able to easily identify your purpose?

Result Orientation

Employees who are keen on achieving results are capable of clearing obstacles from work paths. They engage in planning and optimization to obtain a meaningful return on investment. Their methods are fact based as well as intuitive. They have an in-depth knowledge of their field and industry. They know how things work. They prefer quantifiable measurements to vague objectives. They are eager to resolve stalled or irretrievable projects as quickly as possible. They invest themselves in the challenge at hand. They are capable of regrouping after recognizing the red flags. They are adept at taking another approach when necessary. They brainstorm till the answer seems obvious. They ask for feedback.

- Do you hold yourself accountable for realizing results?
- Do you have a clear understanding of all the variables?
- Do you analyze all your options?
- Do you minimize risks but initiate action?
- Do you adhere to high standards to propel favorable outcomes?
- Do you listen to what others have to say?
- Do you consider how a good decision affects you, your coworkers, and your organization?
- Do you consider how a difficult decision affects you, your coworkers, your supervisor, and your organization?
- Do you set reasonable goals to achieve your aims?
- Do you reward yourself and others once those goals are achieved?
- Do you seek your coworkers' support?
- Do you manage your time well so that you can review your progress as you move through each step of the process?
- Are you eager to stretch your abilities?
- Do you build a consensus to achieve your results?
- Do you carefully consider how your performance impacts the organization as a whole?

Accountability

Employees who are accountable pride themselves on their work and take responsibility for projects, objectives, or events even when they go awry. They treat everyone—vendors, customers, clients, investors, coworkers—fairly. They do not hide bad results. They embrace transparency. They never point fingers. They take responsibility for their actions and decisions. They respond to their critics—

both internally and externally—truthfully. They continually improve standards. They adhere to these standards even when they are tested. They regulate themselves first. They offer fair wages and benefits, or they work hard for the wages and benefits they receive. They produce quality, competitively priced products and/or services.

- Do you refrain from blaming others?
- Do you avoid classifying yourself as a victim?
- Do you ask yourself how you can improve next time around if the results were less than what you expected?
- Are you capable of admitting you are wrong?
- Do you aspire to excellence?
- Do you play fairly?
- Are you more interested in the company's objectives than your own agenda?
- Do you respect confidentiality but refuse to hide the truth?
- Do you continually improve best practices and standards?
- Do you abide by the same rules that you expect everyone else to adhere to?
- Do you welcome competition but win fairly?
- Do you share credit when warranted?
- Do you take responsibility when a project or new direction nose-dives?

Relentless Pursuit of Quality

Employees who relentlessly pursue quality ensure that their products and/or services continually exceed expectations. Excellence is the guiding value. They do not cut corners or lower standards to achieve their aims. They are committed to offering the best in the marketplace. They are competitive but continually raising the bar. They are other-focused instead of self-centered. They are tireless and self-motivated. They take pride in their output. They accurately assess a situation before they begin to improve it.

- Do you continually choose to excel?
- Do you welcome opportunities to improve and streamline?
- Are you committed to your work?
- Do you assess situations realistically?
- Do you admire a job done well even if it's done by the competition?
- Do you learn from your mistakes?
- Do you have an in-depth knowledge of your business and your industry?

- Are you capable of identifying a better method to achieve your results?
- Do you consider opposing viewpoints objectively?
- Do you welcome debate and brainstorming?
- Do you ask for feedback from your customers/clients?
- Do you ask a lot of questions?
- Are you energized by a challenge?
- Do you congratulate yourself and others on a well-done job?

Innovation

Employees who innovate are perennial students. They remain open and committed to value-added products, services, systems, methodologies, and practices. They are always on the lookout for new ideas. They are intuitive and confident of their abilities. They acknowledge risk but move forward. They devour and process information until a pattern or truth is revealed. They are not overly committed to the mousetrap they invented yesterday. They continually improve and streamline.

- Do you read and research voraciously?
- Do you develop strategies and methodologies to discover new ideas?
- Are you curious and engaged by your work?
- Are you forward thinking?
- Do you chart a course to better identify robust developments in your business and industry?
- Are you capable of building a consensus so business units embark on new ventures?
- Do you drive an idea or concept with business potential to its logical conclusion?
- Are you open and articulate with strategies and methodologies so that the necessary business units can jump on board?
- Do you recognize cross-functional applications?
- Do you set a premium on your credibility within the organization?
- Do you continually test prototypes?
- Are you teachable?
- Are you rigorous in exploring integration plans?

Enthusiasm for the Job

Employees who are enthusiastic about their work have a positive, can-do approach toward daily responsibilities and workload. They make recommendations for improvement. They are engaged by what they do. Their enthusiasm is contagious. They are advocates of peer learning and mentoring. Their enthusiasm propels them to tackle more difficult projects. They are eager to be challenged by bigger projects and more complex implementations.

- Are you eager to begin new projects?
- Do you anticipate potential problems and develop contingency plans to avert trouble?
- Do you have a go-getting personality?
- Do you volunteer for projects that stretch your capabilities?
- Do you create and foster an environment that encourages all employees?
- Do you stay abreast of issues and developments that are relevant to your industry or customers?
- Are you a vision builder?
- Do you display effort and attention to whatever is required?
- Are you versatile and flexible?
- Do you feel connected to your company's mission?
- Do you periodically renegotiate your role within the group?
- Do you exhibit decisiveness even under adverse circumstances?
- Do you support valuable contributions made by others?
- Do you lead by attraction rather than promotion?
- Do you offer guidance and support to those who are less inclined to move forward?
- Do you balance day-to-day routine responsibilities with engaging activities?
- Do you remain optimistic in collaborative projects that are languishing?

Flexibility

Employees who are flexible are on the lookout for new and better ideas. They are not rigid nor are they overly committed to routine procedure. They fix what's broken while simultaneously considering the ramifications. They recognize emerging trends. They are skilled at handling transitions. They do not punch their way into a corner. They adapt to ever-increasing changes—whether in the economy or in the workplace. They let go of outdated procedures without rancor.

They are intrigued by the next big thing. They embrace diversity and challenge—and can bounce back under stressful conditions.

- Do you remain open to new ideas or procedures?
- Are you inclusive in your dealings with others?
- Do you adapt to new technologies and practices?
- Do you sign up for training?
- Do you keep abreast of new developments and trends?
- Are you inventive and creative?
- Can you go in a new direction when necessary?
- Do you consider change an opportunity?
- Do you position yourself to adapt to change?
- Do you acquire new skills readily?
- Can you identify win-win opportunities?
- Do you look at all the alternatives?
- Are you forward thinking?
- Are you resilient?

Diplomacy

Employees who exhibit diplomacy are tactful and discreet. They do not bully or manipulate. They are committed to building a consensus. They have a patient understanding of process. They do not offend or belittle to get their way. Their communication is clear, firm, and honest. They give people an out when necessary. They collaborate and help others. They do not publicly criticize others. They resolve conflicts rationally and by going through the chain of command. They do not react in anger. They pause. They are considerate of morale. They observe protocol.

- Do you value relationship over getting your own way?
- Do you refrain from negativity and ego-bruising criticism?
- Do you acknowledge the benefit of remaining calm during a crisis?
- Do you listen with open ears to a difference of opinion?
- Do you deal with problems rather than expect others to take care of them?
- Do you keep everyone informed of decisions that affect them?
- Do you see all sides?
- Are you courteous?
- Do you validate others for a well-done job?
- Are you inclusive and generous when coming to a decision?

- Can you see the humorous side of things when events are veering out of control?

Motivation in Seeking the Job

Job seekers who are motivated to get hired do their research and study their business and industry. They recognize openings before they are posted by following industry news and trends. They seek the necessary information to make good matches with companies. They are not easily deflated. They bounce back quickly from rejection. They develop marketable skills. They follow procedures and/or protocol. They prepare for their interviews and make an effort to put forth their best selves. They are interested in the company that they want to work for, and they show a commitment to their work and/or careers.

- Do you continually hone and polish your skills?
- Are you teachable?
- Are you willing to adapt to your surroundings to better serve yourself, your coworkers, and your employer?
- Do you investigate opportunities to make an inroad into a particular company?
- Do you network to broaden your job opportunities?
- Do you stay abreast of current technological developments?
- Are you committed to developing and enhancing your can-do attitude?
- Are you getting the necessary experience—through internships or by shadowing or volunteering—to transition into the workplace steadily?
- Do you invest in continual learning opportunities?
- Do you enroll in classes that further your objectives?
- Do you target particular companies and then figure out ways to make inroads into those companies?
- Are you eager to prove yourself?
- Do you have a willingness to do what it takes to become successful in your field?
- Are you willing to exhibit effort and determination?
- Have you thoughtfully considered all your career options?
- Do you have a plan, strategy, or course laid out to implement your objectives?

BUILDING EMPLOYMENT MUSCLE

The previous 23 personal qualities were listed by the Fortune 500 respondents. Meeting those expectations may seem like a tall order. Don't feel overwhelmed. No one—no matter how qualified and self-motivated—has all of these qualities. In fact, some qualities would be unsuitable for particular positions, and some companies place more emphasis on certain attributes over others. The intention was to provide a specific list so that you know what Fortune 500 companies value (and most likely smaller companies as well).

Look at the language used to describe these attributes and examine how they relate to your own working persona. Addressing these attributes—or at least the ones you already have—will be helpful in your interview as well as in your career. In fact, you might want to consider this list as a guideline for your professional development. Think of it as 23 ways to improve your work self. Ed Koch, the former mayor of New York City, used to ask at his press conferences, "How am I doing?" That's a good question to ask every day. How are you doing? At home, at work, and in life? And then the next question: How can I do better?

8

THE QUESTIONS FORTUNE 500 EMPLOYERS ASK

"My questions are behavioral/situational based and vary by position. I develop a list of questions for each position I am interviewing for and then ask the same questions of all applicants for that position."

ANNE FOOTE COLLINS
Director of Corporate Recruiting and Services
Office Depot, Inc.

One way to ensure a good outcome at your interview is to answer the interviewer's questions thoroughly and insightfully. You may be wondering how you can prepare for an interview for a specific job at a specific company armed with the information you read in this chapter. In one sense, you can never be 100 percent prepared for the questions you will be asked at *your* interview. So much depends on the particular company and the nature of the job you will be expected to perform. Even if your interview opens with some general questions, eventually you have to address the specifics regarding how you are qualified for that particular job.

But you can get a fairly accurate sense of how you are going to be quizzed by looking at some of the questions that Fortune 500 hiring managers utilize during their interviews. The average interview lasts about an hour, and you can expect to be probed in those 60 minutes. Even when an interviewer runs out of standard questions, the conversation may not be over. When concluding an interview at TIAA-CREF, Moll asks candidates, "What haven't I asked you that you would like to tell me about?"

Whether you plan to work for an energetic start-up or a corporate titan, it's valuable to know what Fortune 500 hiring managers ask their job applicants. These colossal companies set the bar—and it's high—so give yourself a running start. Think about how you would answer these questions at your interview and, by all means, build your own responses. When you review the Fortune 500 questions, think about your job, your work history, your strength and skills, what personal attributes you can bring to a new position, and how you can make a positive impact at the new company. Remember to be specific and use examples.

THE FORTUNE 500 QUESTIONS

1. What are you looking for ideally in a job?
2. Tell me about how you got to where you are.
3. We have a number of very talented applicants for this position. Why should we select you?
4. Tell me a little bit about yourself.
5. What area needs personal and professional development?
6. Why did you major in X?
7. Why are you leaving X Company?
8. Tell me about a specific project you recently worked on.
9. If I talked to your manager, what would he or she tell me about you?
10. What interests you about *this* job at *this* company?
11. What did you learn from one of the projects that you worked on that failed?
12. If you could recreate one cultural aspect from a previous employer and bring it here, what would it be?
13. Describe your wow factor to me.
14. Have you acquired a reputation for anything in your work?
15. What competencies would you like us to help you develop?
16. What leader do you admire most? Why? What have you learned from that person?
17. What have your accomplishments been in your current role?
18. What are your career aspirations in both the short term and the long term?
19. What influenced you to pursue a career in your particular area of expertise?
20. Why is this position your next right move?
21. Tell me about your qualifications and what experiences/skills you can bring to this organization that will add value?
22. Why did you go to X College?
23. What is motivating you in considering another position?
24. Explain to me a situation in which your business and personal ethics were challenged. Describe it, and how did you respond to it?
25. Describe your leadership style.

HOW TO ANSWER THE QUESTIONS

Remember what PepsiCo's Neil Bussell said: "I've been interviewed more times than I care to remember . . . but you still have to put things in the best light." No matter how difficult the question, your replies must emphasize the positive and cast your work history "in the best light." Even if you have to account for a gap in your work history or a layoff, portray it in the best terms. Allied's O'Leary said, "Be honest about the gap, but explain how you took advantage of the time off." Everyone experiences downturns in their life. Most employers are more interested in how you bounced back from them.

So look the interviewer in the eye, sit up straight, and observe the cues (a nod, a yawn, maybe paper shuffling, or even a big smile). These signals give you some idea whether you are on the right track, and then be responsive to the cues. Speak clearly, and try not to sound as though you have memorized a script. Be prepared to switch your focus if the interviewer seems impatient or bored or negative. But always try to be as natural as you can . . . under the circumstances. Timken's Barry Martin said candidates often stumble when he asks them for a brief overview of their career—"People tend to talk way too much"—so remember to be sensitive to the interviewer's time. Be clear, be thoughtful, and be confident.

How Would You Answer . . . ?

The following responses to the questions highlight various professions, but the bulleted points afterward should show you what to emphasize and how to relate these answers to your own background. When you speak, try to keep the tone conversational and friendly at all times. Employers are trying to gauge your skills, but they are also evaluating whether you have the right personality to fit in with the group or department.

1. What are you looking for ideally in a job?

Reply (Computer Programmer): I have ten years' experience as a programmer analyst, so I have a good sense of my strengths and what I need from a job. Even though I am very focused on data, working in a team environment suits my personality. Ideally, my coworkers will energize me. I like working on a team because it gives me an opportunity to learn different styles and next-generation technologies. In my last job the team consisted of eight programmers. Each of us brought something different, yet strong, to the table. I remember one project where we couldn't decide which database technology we needed to use in this very complicated migration project. One coworker wanted to use Sybase, another Oracle, another DB2. We had long, heated discussions about our options. I came away from those debates energized and excited. I felt as though I was learning all the time.

After thinking about my next career move, I decided—after working for the two smaller companies I mentioned earlier—that ideally I want to be working for a large, reputable company. Affiliation has always been important to me. Your company has a stable, yet strong, market presence in Internet-based systems. Web hosting and data analysis are my strong points. The possibilities in this field are infinite, so I would like to work in an environment where my inventiveness is encouraged. For the most part, I want to spend my day engaged in Internet-based applications but also in an environment with other programmers where there is a lot of give-and-take. That would be ideal.

- You want to convey first and foremost that you have spent some time thinking about your career. Remember when presidential hopeful Ted Kennedy was asked by Roger Mudd why he wanted to be President? At first he appeared dumbfounded, and then he wavered and mumbled something incoherent. It was obvious to the live television audience that Senator Kennedy didn't spend too much time thinking about why he wanted the most important job in the country. He did not get the job.

- Show that you have a comfort level in your field, yet at the same time refrain from technospeak and jargon (which would alienate the interviewer if his or her background is not the same as yours). So be specific, but also be clear. Provide examples and use carefully chosen words. Try to keep your responses conversational in tone.

- Convey your enthusiasm for your work and your excitement about the prospect of continuing it in an even more challenging and robust environment—the company where you are interviewing. Try to incorporate into your responses what you have already learned about the company during the interview process.

- You have an opportunity in your responses to emphasize your accomplishments and strengths—again and again—regardless of whether you are addressing that point or not. Feel free to incorporate information you previously covered—such as your aptitude in various computer programs—for the purpose of emphasis or illustration. Highlighting these strengths leaves a good impression.

- Keep in mind the company values and the necessary requirements for the specific job. The Fortune 500 respondents' input suggests that personality is also a key factor. If you know for a fact that you will be working on a team, show the interviewer that you are adept at working within one. If you know that the company values innovation (perhaps it was mentioned in its mission statement), then show how that strength relates to you (provided, of course, you *are* inventive).

- The crux of the job interview is the Q&A. It's all about how you answer the questions and the kind of questions you ask the employer. According to Lara Crane, a manager of staffing at Alltel, applicants would be wise to "learn from the interview. Use this time to do a self-evaluation and set goals. Interviews often help you become more confident with your skill set and abilities. Examine what you have, what you want, and how you want to improve yourself."

2. Tell me about how you got to where you are.

Reply (Sales Manager): As you can see by my résumé, like everybody else directly out of college, I started at the bottom as a sales representative at GVBC. I did print advertising and conducted outside sales with the local businesses in the community. I did well, but there were periods of the month when I was hungry. So I created my own business doing promotion for local bars and clubs at night. It took off, and I managed to bring 500 to 1,200 people into those clubs on a regular basis. In fact, I built the company from the ground up, hired a few people, and I was able to leave my day job. I also had enough extra revenue to finish my masters.

A few of my business associates suggested I go to ENT, Inc. because it was a fast-growing company with lots of opportunity. I think I was hired by that company because of my strong sales background and communications skills. I also have a knack for cultivating new clients and expanding territories. I have been with ENT for five years now. It's a good company. In one way the growth at ENT reminds me of your company, but on another level I think you offer something that ENT cannot provide: stability and more opportunity to advance.

But back to ENT, I was promoted quickly. I continually exceeded expectations. In my first year I won two of the four company-wide sales contests. I then won a Top Performer Award in the fourth quarter. This moved me up to senior account executive the following year—in April actually. I just want to mention here that I achieved my sales goals 83 percent of time while at ENT. The next few years I focused on building relationships with national, especially New York, advertising agencies. I was consistently rewarded raises because I accomplished my goals. Last year I was promoted again to sales manager, as I was ranked Number One East Coast Salesman and also generated 21 percent of *all* sales in 2004. I am a go-getter, and I am very adept at listening to clients' needs so that good relationships develop. That's a quick overview, but basically that's how I got to where I am today.

- Do not hesitate to relate on a human level. Try to build a rapport with the interviewer. At one point in his or her career, the interviewer has been where you are now. Employers are more interested in your progression than they are in where you started, so always highlight promotions and advancement.

- You want to emphasize, especially for a sales position, that you know how to build and maintain relationships and that you have good communication skills. Reviewing your résumé several times before an interview helps you to speak precisely and fluidly about what is listed (the particulars of your work history, in other words, won't trip you up).

- Make a connection between what you did and what you plan to do. That's why drawing comparisons between the company you worked for and the company where you want to work makes sense. If the position you are seeking is entirely different from the job you had, then emphasize your ability to learn quickly and your eagerness to be challenged.

- Speak positively about your past employer and job—no matter what. Naturally the prospective employer knows you are not entirely satisfied with your current position (otherwise you would not be seeking a new job), but it is never acceptable to lambaste a former employer or job. Complaining about your current position provides the new employer with two telling details: you are negative and you may say the same thing about this employer somewhere down the line. It is acceptable to say that the new position offers you something that the old one does not—as long as that something is not more money or shorter hours or less responsibility or anything else that suggests you are more interested in getting than giving (even if one of these factors *is* the reason you are looking for a new job).

- Your answers are better when they are thorough but not long-winded. Most interviews last approximately an hour, and a lot of information needs to be covered. Do not become so verbose that you lose the interviewer's attention. Again, it's essential you pay attention to the signals. Of course, how much time you spend on each question depends on what you want to emphasize. Brevity serves you well if the question is not remotely applicable to your experience or background. Just remember that at a later point in the interview you have to expand to guarantee that the interviewer gets a good sense of who you are and what you have to offer.

- Be specific and provide examples. Numbers tell a better story than does hype. If you are going to say you are "the best in the business," provide some figures to back you up. Allied's O'Leary said, "Be prepared to provide specific relevant examples with quantifiable results."

3. We have a number of very talented applicants for this position. Why should we select you?

Reply (Magazine Editor): I have a diverse background with experience in many facets of production and content development. I have worked on both sides of the editorial process—as a writer and editor—so I am a better manager because I understand the process so thoroughly. In addition I think I'm ready for another challenge. I have always been a reader of this magazine, and I admire its focus and content. As an editor I have a good sense of emerging trends. It's something I have always enjoyed about this business—being a few months ahead of the curve. Knowing what's about to come out on the market—whether it's a new movie, product, book, or fashion—is a big plus.

Another strength that makes me particularly suited to this position is that I am at my best when faced with tight deadlines. I am proud of the fact that in the five years I've been at BCD, I have never missed a deadline. You mentioned that the pace at this company can be frenetic. This is the type of atmosphere where I do my best work, as I prefer working in a high-energy environment. I am much more effective when there isn't too much downtime.

I also like the fact that I will be working with the managing editor on content as well as production. At my last position, I spent a lot of time ensuring that the proofreading, editing, and style guidelines were in place. I enjoy all aspects of production, but I would like to shift my focus toward content. I am an excellent fact-checker, researcher, and copy editor, so assigning articles seems like the next logical step. As a voracious reader, I have a good feel for the marketplace. I think this is helpful when developing ideas. Your company has a reputation for moving out way ahead of the curve. I like your shorter lead time and quick production cycle. That way you can cover breaking news sooner.

In my research, I noticed my skills were a good match for the position. I am thoroughly familiar with CMS and Quark. And I noticed in the job posting that editors must know *The Chicago Manual of Style* inside out. I am well versed in that stylebook, which makes me a more effective editor for freelancers, who are not so familiar with the magazine's style. I also know AP style because of my newspaper background. I think I'm the perfect fit for this position.

- You may have heard of keywords in relationship to writing your résumé. Well, keywords also apply to talking about the prospective job. Review the job description—whether it was on the company Web site or in a classified ad in the newspaper—and highlight those words that represent the skills required for the job. Speak to those skills when you answer the questions. It's another way to reinforce that you are qualified and comfortable with what the new job requires.

- Convey that you like your work and are interested in the business. Show an understanding of the industry. It shows focus and interest. In addition, your interest is a good sign that you will be in the job for the long haul. Replacing an employee is costly and time consuming.

- Move back and forth between your experience and what you know about the new job, but emphasize other personal attributes as well. If you are skilled at meeting deadlines, mention it (even if you are not sure how tight the deadlines will be). If you have a detailed plan for achieving your career goals, throw that into the mix as well.

- You should refer to the research you have done. Prefacing your statements with such openers as "I noticed on your Web site . . ." or "I read in your annual report . . ." emphasizes you have done your homework. When you invest your time in research, it implies you are serious about the job as well as your future prospects.

- Remember to save some information for follow-up. After your initial response, there's a good chance that the interviewer will ask you to provide more specifics to determine the depth of your experience, so be prepared to talk in detail about any salient points that are particularly relevant to the new job. One Fortune 500 staffing manager said, "Most candidates stumble after probing for specifics from [the] initial response. They have difficulty explaining the relevance of their actions."

4. Tell me a little bit about yourself.

Reply (Accountant): After graduating from ABC College, I began as an accountant at D&L, where I spent most of my time analyzing quarterly and yearly financial statement balances. Occasionally I worked on client portfolios and composed audit reports. It was my first introduction to the business and I liked the work, but I wanted more diversification, so I returned to school and got my MBA in finance at NU. I am really glad I spent some time at D&L before going back for my MBA. By the time I went to ARD, which was an interim step for me while I completed my masters, I had a good idea of what direction to follow. The telecom boom was at its height when I was at ARD, so I was knee-deep in daily client reports on telecom services and equipment. My reports focused on projections of equity prices. Those were heady times, very exciting—change was minute-by-minute practically. Oh, yes, at ARD I also constructed quantitative models for earnings and equity valuations.

With my background in sell-side equity research, I made a move to TDS, which was a significant step up for me. At TDS, I was a member of several four-person deal teams. We did a lot of due diligence, credit analyses, some negotiation of transaction terms and loan documentations. I spent quite a bit of time with investors. I am very persuasive, and I was adept at convincing investors to jump on board several key initiatives. Two years ago, I was promoted to Transaction Manager. I currently have 13 accounts worth $600 million in the media and communications portfolio. Recently I negotiated two loan defaults of Argentine cable companies. I am happy to report that the negotiation resulted in a partial receipt of interest payments and loan principal. The company—and particularly my supervisor—considered the negotiation very successful. I noticed your company is the most geographically dispersed accounting firm. I have a great deal of international experience and am fluent in Spanish and proficient in French.

As for outside work, I am busy renovating a co-op I recently bought downtown. I recently moved into the city and am thrilled to be here, even though I don't know who the good plumbers or contractors are yet.

- You want to provide a mix of hard skills/soft skills when describing the work you did at a former position, especially if you are speaking to someone not directly involved in the department where you will be working—provided you get the job. Balance the qualifications necessary for the new position (for instance, negotiating loan defaults) with softer skills that the interviewer can understand and relate to (for instance, adeptness at persuasion). You may lose the interviewer's interest if you go off on technical know-how tangents.
- An interviewer asking to know a "little more about you" means he or she wants to get to know who you are primarily in your work life (not necessar-

ily what you did last Saturday night). Although you should not totally neglect your personal life and interests, they definitely take a back seat to your work life.

- Some career experts suggest you memorize one joke before your interview. If telling a joke is part of who you are (and the joke is not off-color), then feel free to slip one in at the appropriate moment—provided you are fairly certain it would be received well. A spontaneous response or touch of humor is more effective, however, than is a memorized joke. Remember the job applicant in Chapter 5 who said, "Next question, doctor."

- All experience is good experience—as long as you see it in the "best light." Even if your first job out of college was, for the most part, excruciating, emphasize what good came out of it (for instance, you returned to school and got another degree). Adjust your attitude so you recognize that mistakes are merely stepping stones, or as jazz musician Miles Davis once said, "Do not fear mistakes. There are none."

- Interviewers are skilled conversationalists. The best bet is to be somewhat reserved or circumspect and not mistake their friendliness as an invitation to become effusive. They do not want your whole life story. Instead, provide only the information that is relevant to your work life. One Fortune 500 director of strategic staffing said, "For me, it's important to establish that we find out what brought the candidates here. What do they find really compelling? My interview isn't really a back and forth. It's behavioral . . . a conversation to make them comfortable so they will share with me. And they do. I get them to share a lot."

5. What area needs personal and professional development?

Reply (Reporter): I move very quickly. I think it has a lot to do with working in this business ten years—breaking news and deadlines. Where I may need some improvement is in my expectations that others will move as quickly as I do. I sometimes feel impatient when things must go through endless channels for approval. Of course, I never let my displeasure show, but I must admit that I am always wondering why things don't unfold at a much faster pace. Part of the problem is that I work project to project. I write one article, and I am on to the next—always investigating the next newsworthy event—so I can be single-mindedly focused and not have enough understanding of those who are continually multifocused. This is an area in which I know I must lower my expectations—not so much for their sake but for mine. That way I won't be disappointed the next time someone tells me they will get back to me . . . in two weeks. On the other hand, I don't think I would be such a good reporter if I weren't so single-minded. It drives me to dig, dig, dig. But I should be more sensitive to the kind of environment others work in, where there are a lot of interests competing for their time.

- This answer works—provided that the job posting did not state that the applicant must have to wade through various organizational levels to get things done. That's why it's imperative you parse the job posting and look at the company Web site to make sure you understand (as much as humanly possible) what is required to perform the new job in a new corporate culture.
- Fitting a square peg into a round hole characterizes a lot of job interviews. That's why you should not take it personally when you are not hired for a particular job. Hiring managers have a good idea of what it takes to be successful in a particular job—information that you may never uncover, even after doing hours and hours of research, so trust the system. Alltel's Crane advises applicants to "keep applying. Just because you don't get one job, doesn't mean that you won't get another."
- Even with probing questions that target your professional *and* personal life, you must still focus primarily on your work life. This is a job interview, not a psychiatrist's office, so be judicious and tread carefully. Just provide enough personal information to show that you are a capable *employee* and a decent human being.
- Again, cast everything in the best light. You don't want to suggest that you are blind to your faults, but, at the same time, you don't want to imply that you are difficult to work with either. A single-minded reporter may be just what the company needs, even though that single focus is causing the reporter a little chagrin.

6. Why did you major in X?

Reply (Biologist): The first semester I was at college, I was convinced I wanted to be a veterinarian. I grew up with two dogs, three cats, and an assortment of other small critters. So I took a lot of biology classes—on animal behavior, marine biology, plant systematics—and then I took a class on genetics that basically changed my whole direction. It may have had something to do with the professor, who was phenomenal, but suddenly I found myself more interested in human applications than in animals. I knew I had made the right decision after a few more classes with that professor. She actually helped me find an internship and also refocused my major. She was very influential. I consider her an important mentor for me while I was at school.

I know I'm just starting out, but I think I have a lot to offer your company. I am a strong writer too, so I was hoping to use this skill in a multi-disciplinary manner. Without totally getting away from clinical trials, running instruments, and other bench work that I got a taste of during my internship at YZ Pharmaceuticals, I would also like to work on reports with other scientists for, say, the Food and Drug Administration. I enjoy collaborative projects and I know the science already, so the technical background will have a real impact on my ability to communicate. I thoroughly enjoyed my major in college and feel confident I am in the right field. I recently read an article in the *Job Rated Almanac* that ranked a biology career as the "Best-Rated Job." Many, many courses later, I feel comfortable with my focus.

- Emphasizing your ability to communicate effectively is always a plus with employers. Most employees work in groups or teams at larger companies—so the ability to communicate in that type of collaborative environment is essential. Add to that good writing skills, and you become a very desirable employee. Today you can't escape the fact that you work in the Information Age. Being able to process lots of information and put it into readable form is a great asset.

- Conveying an enthusiasm for your field of study is a good indication that you will be satisfied in your job—provided, of course, there is some relationship between your field of study and your job. If there is no relationship, then de-emphasize your coursework and instead focus on the new territory you would like to explore.

- Mentoring is a highly regarded concept in business. Whether you recognize it or not, at one time it is likely that someone took you under his or her care and helped you. Think about the people who have helped you in your career or academic/athletic life, and acknowledge that help if it is relevant.

- Recent graduates cannot rely on their experience, so they should focus on their potential. Talking about your career game plan gives the employer an idea of the direction you want to go as well as a glimpse at what drives you as an employee. Your optimism is appreciated. One Fortune 500 staffing manager advised applicants: "Be positive, smile, and demonstrate your value." But BellSouth's Snypp warns: "Be confident but not egotistical." Talk about real skills that you have rather than what a great person you are.

- Always emphasize your capability to be a team player. In today's business environment, it's guaranteed that you will be working closely with others—and relationship building is key to how successful your projects/work will be.

7. Why are you leaving **X** company?

Reply (Office Manager to Publicist): Actually, as an office manager my intention was to round out my skills. At my first job out of college, I was an assistant director at an art gallery, where I utilized my background in fine arts. Although I enjoyed working with the public, writing press releases, and managing day-to-day operations, I discovered that I needed to strengthen some of my other skills. That's why I went to DEF. There I was able to immerse myself in the technology that will further my goals, which is to represent artists and writers in larger markets.

At my current job I develop and maintain databases and tracking sheets as well as grant-related tracking. I also manage the internal news/press cataloging system. I have become involved with Web site maintenance in recent months—a skill I have wanted to develop for a long time—by working closely with the CTO on technical support. He encouraged me to take an HTML night course at the community school, which I have just completed. I think this will help me when I deal with clients who need to know how to place the contents of the media kit on their Web site and thereby allow reporters to access the information instantly.

I see my current position as an excellent stepping stone, but I believe I am ready to use what I have learned so far in all my former jobs—my excellent telephone skills (which were sharpened considerably while at DEF), my media contacts, and event planning—in a position more closely aligned with my interest in the arts. I understand that as a publicist at your firm, I will be working primarily on media kits as well as other publicity campaigns. The success I had at the gallery, where revenue increased 30 percent while I was there, suggests that I have a good understanding of selling emerging trends to the media.

- If you made a lateral move in your career, you may want to downplay your primary responsibilities at your current (or former) job and instead underscore the features that you would like to focus on in your next position. In other words, if you prefer not to maintain databases all day, then don't overemphasize how adept you are at doing precisely this. Instead, focus on the aspects of the current job that you like, even if you spent a small portion of your day performing them. This gives the interviewer a better sense of the direction in which you want to go.

- Quantifiable numbers are always a plus. Saying business improved by 30 percent is better than saying business improved while you were there (provided, of course, it's true). That means you should keep track of how well you performed in your former position (perhaps by reading your most recent performance review). Telling an employer exactly what your impact was while you were at X Company creates a much better impression than spouting off how much you contributed without any hard facts to back you up.

- Do not underestimate the importance of telephone skills. Millions of dollars are lost in businesses each year because employees didn't return telephone calls or associates never made follow-up calls. Effectiveness on the telephone is a prime component of your communication skills.

- As you did on your résumé, don't neglect to mention your computer literacy. Regardless of the profession you are in these days, you need to know the technology related to that field. If you don't have the necessary computer skills for the particular job you are applying for, sign up for a class immediately.

- Despite many variations of this question, there is an excellent chance that you'll be asked at one point in the interview why you are leaving your current position (unless you are a recent graduate). In fact, this is the first question Lara Crane, the staffing manager at Alltel, asks. Crane said, "After introductions and a description of the company and position, we ask about the candidate's current position and the reason he or she is leaving that position."

8. Tell me about a specific project you recently worked on.

Reply (Director of Systems): My last project involved supporting a large equity trading exchange. We had to provide a functional migration from a manually intensive method for brokers on the floor to express their trading interest through an electronic method. Before the migration, brokers on the trading floor orally expressed their interest to the specialists, who had to manually enter that interest into a template at their workstations. This was time consuming for a fast market. The new project, the migration, was intended to allow the brokers to electronically express their interest from their handheld terminals and have their quotes pass through our trading systems and arrive in the specialists' open order book as orders to buy or sell. This streamlined the process considerably.

My role was to coordinate the planning, development, testing, and implementation activities across diverse groups within my company as well as to outside vendors. I had to raise and mitigate issues, report status to senior management, and develop testing methodologies. The major challenge was to ensure a coordinated development effort among these diverse groups and maintain a strict cutover schedule because the project was run under an XXX-mandated delivery time frame. Time to market was of the essence. This new functionality was needed to maintain the SSS's role as the leading marketplace for equity trading.

- Even though your answers should be specific, don't give away any inside information when speaking about your former position and/or company. Confidential information should be protected—even if you are planning to exit the company as soon as possible. Speak only about projects that do not compromise your current company (or impact its competitive edge). You want to convey to your prospective employer that you can be trusted with inside information.
- If your role at your former company was highly technical, always provide some description of your duties in plain English so that interviewers without a technical background can determine the impact of your recent project. Some interviewers will hit the brain's snooze button if technical jargon is interminable.
- Even if you are moving to a different area or field or even career, you still need to be able to provide specific examples of the work you have done, especially your accomplishments. Audrey Goodman, a vice president at Medco Health Solutions, advised: "Be prepared to talk about your work in detail."
- Especially in managerial positions, the *I* takes a back seat to the *we*. Always remember to emphasize your team orientation. Employers are more interested in how you led the team than in how you captured all the glory.
- When asked to describe a recent project, choose a challenging and highly successful project. Spend some time thinking about what obstacles you had to overcome to make this project a success.

9. If I talked to your manager, what would he or she tell me about you?

Reply (Marketing Director): He would say I understand niches well and that I am creative. In addition, my communication skills let me move effortlessly between the newsroom trenches and the boardroom. Those are my major strengths, but he would also emphasize that I know how to sell and also what salespeople need to close the deal. I recently developed highly successful publicity campaigns for our daily newspaper—plus five weeklies—that produce revenue from our niche markets. He would say I have a good understanding of the needs of these diverse markets. The audience for the weeklies includes Latinos, other immigrant populations, African Americans, artists, and young professionals. In addition, for the weeklies I provided writing, editorial, and creative concepts. Advertising pages have doubled in the last three months.

My supervisor would say that my leadership skills are excellent as well. I lead a team of eight writers and artists for the five weeklies—creative members notorious for following their own individual lead—and we produce a cohesive and revenue-building lineup for our company. To top it off, we consistently come in on budget and on schedule.

- The marketplace, as well as the workplace, is diverse. Do not hesitate to mention your aptitude for navigating amid this diversity as well as your understanding of the needs of diverse populations. Businesses have acknowledged that their workplaces must adequately mirror the marketplace to remain competitive.

- Think about what your current supervisor would say about you. If you don't know, look at your performance review, or ask. Does it match how you see yourself? Portray yourself in realistic terms. Seeing yourself clearly is a good indication that you are self-reflective, thoughtful, and objective. Don't pretend you are something you are not. If you are by nature a pistol-toting maverick and you sense the prospective employer values team players, resist the temptation to play into an expectation for the sake of an offer. You won't be making a good match—and you may end up repeating this whole process sooner than you would like.

- Always expect to follow up any of your responses with additional information. Perhaps something you said piques the interviewer's attention. Be prepared to provide additional detail. That's why you should not be too eager to put all of your information on the table at one shot. Keep your responses concise, and elaborate when asked.

- Staying within budget and meeting deadlines—as pedestrian as that may sound to you when describing your responsibilities—are of keen interest to most employers. Remember to keep in mind what an employer values, even if other features or aspects of your former position are more worthy of note to you.

- For more senior positions, one Fortune 500 participant opens her interview with questions about management style: "I do like to see how people react to the question about managing people. I'll ask them about their skills at managing. The kind of responses I get are really telling."

10. What interests you about *this* job at *this* company?

Reply (HR Generalist): I am a good fit for this position, and there are several aspects of this job that interest me. X Corporation is an international company with a diverse workforce. I am fluent is Polish and Spanish, so I think this fluency will be useful in day-to-day employee relations. I also hope to work closely with your global staffing and recruitment departments. I noticed this company provides many opportunities for advancement. And you mentioned your policy of promoting internally before you look outside the company to fill key positions.

I have a bachelor's degree in psychology, so this background should prove useful in your Employee Career Development Department, which directs many initiatives on training, safety, and counseling. I have excellent communication skills, and I am particularly adept at conflict management and problem solving, especially if I am called on to referee disputes between mismatched employees.

In my last position in the personnel department of BDC, I was often called on to deliver presentations on various training modules, especially safety issues. And I certainly can be trusted with confidentiality issues. In addition, I noticed on your Web site that the position requires a familiarity with both Microsoft Office and PeopleSoft. I am thoroughly proficient with Microsoft, and I did use PeopleSoft for expense accounts in my last position, so I think the transition to this new job at X Corporation will be quick and smooth. I am also familiar with many of your internal protocols. Your Reward Plan, which complements overall compensation based on the performance of the company, is impressive. I think this instills in workers the value of teamwork by rewarding them financially when they meet or exceed goals. And your FlexPlan that seeks to retain people who may leave to spend time with their families is also innovative.

My fluency in languages and excellent interpersonal skills will add a lot of value to your department. Plus your innovative programs and comprehensive employee services will provide me with plenty of room to grow and advance. I am eager to become a part of your staff because of this innovation.

- This question cannot be answered thoroughly unless you have invested some time researching both the company and the position. A cursory glance at the Web site is not sufficient. Look at the company's mission statement, look at its Career Page, look at its management structure (and memorize some of the names of key personnel), look at its products and services. Finally, look at how the company describes the position you are interviewing for, and make sure that you use some of the keywords in your own responses (provided, of course, that you do have these skills).

- Whether the question directly addresses your qualifications or not, don't hesitate to mention them in your responses—several times, if necessary, to highlight your strengths and skills. If you're planning to work for an international company, your fluency in language is relevant. If you know that one of the job requirements requires a proficiency in specific computer software, mention your proficiency.

- Strive for specifics. The "I heard it's a great company" response is outdated and too general to have an impact on a hiring manager. You must demonstrate, or sell, your interest in the specific company and job. You need the facts to convey this interest, but don't ramble on and on. When Timken's Barry Martin asks for a "brief overview of your career," he really wants you to be concise "and focus on those experiences that are most related to the position at hand."

- Your interest in advancement suggests to the hiring manager that you are planning to stay at a company for the long haul. You are focused and have developed a career strategy. Employee turnover is an expensive proposition, so your long-term plans are relevant to a prospective employer.

11. What did you learn from one of the projects that you worked on that failed?

Reply (Facilities Manager): I decided to put a full-scale ergonomics into place back in 1997. Just as we were seriously considering the implementation, I started to receive a lot of literature from a small company that offered good prices and all-around service: evaluations, safety plans, and the like. The literature from this company intrigued me—the brochures, the regular correspondence, the press releases—and over the course of the next few months we began to establish a relationship with this new supplier.

At first we ordered piecemeal, and I was quite satisfied with the products and services, and then we jumped on board for a complete installation of keyboard trays, height adjustable workstations, and so on. The supplier was very enthusiastic, and he had worked with some large outfits.

As it turned out, the investment of time was considerable, and the supplier bit off more than he could chew. We had a contract, but there still were serious delays and setbacks. He was a nice guy and I sympathized . . . to a point, but then we basically had to rethink our whole program and supplement products and installations from a different supplier to meet all the specifications. Luckily the new supplier supplemented what the smaller company could not do within the time constraints that we had agreed on. We eventually implemented a very successful ergonomics program after a few sleepless nights, but the experience with the initial supplier taught me a valuable lesson.

I usually buy only from suppliers in which the relationship is a long-standing one—built after many years in this business. But comprehensive ergonomics programs that addressed the needs of the computer workstation were relatively new. I got caught up in the newness of it all and didn't recognize that the scope of this project was too large for a small vendor. Normally I would seek recommendations from other managers in my network, but in this instance I bought into the initial supplier's enthusiasm and was lured by the better prices, hard sell, and sleek marketing materials. I took full responsibility for the delays and am happy we could rescue the project. I manage risk well, but from that point on, I resolved to proceed with even more caution with new vendors and new practices, especially for large-scale projects without tried-and-true comparisons.

The good news is that my company was one of the first to have a full-fledged ergonomics program in place. That risk I don't regret because our workers' compensation claims declined. We reduced workplace injuries considerably by putting the program in as early as we did.

- You may be wondering how to remain positive when asked to describe a project that failed. Ducking this question by saying none of your projects ever failed would imply that you are being untrue or suffering from a bad case of denial, or you are very inexperienced. Think about some projects that were full of obstacles and didn't turn out as well as you hoped they would; consider what you learned in the process and how that experience makes you a better employee now as a result.
- Stay honest, but emphasize your strengths as well. Consider your contingency plan and what you came up with to resolve the matter as you were experiencing these obstacles.
- Take responsibility. Blaming a failure on external events or your coworkers will not further your cause. Accountability is an attribute that is highly rated by the respondents of the Fortune 500 survey. At International Truck

& Engine, *accountability* is one of the company's "seven guiding values" and is also a fair indicator of your level of maturity.

- End the discussion on a positive note. Focus on what you learned or the good outcome that was not evident initially. Always ask yourself what good came out of a bad situation.

12. If you could recreate one cultural aspect from a previous company and bring it here, what would it be?

Reply (Equity Sales Trader): The environment at Corporation X is rigorous. We work long hours, weekends even, and the standards are extremely high. But there is a real emphasis on teamwork and community focus. Regardless of the strong work ethic and high expectations at Corporation X, we are encouraged to participate in CommunityTeam. In fact, last year I was given a week off to volunteer at the local Head Start Program. You tend to get caught up in the daily high-pressure responsibilities of your job, and the time off refreshed me and gave me a better perspective. I had to tackle different issues and reach out on a level that was way out of my comfort zone. I certainly learned how to communicate in the simplest terms—liquidity and supply/demand don't have much meaning to children who are struggling to get their basic needs met. I felt good about the service I provided. I also appreciated the fact that a company as rigorous and demanding as X takes its responsibility to the community seriously. Even though the company donates significantly on a philanthropic level, it also moves beyond just dollars and cents. We invest our time in the community, and then the community gets a better idea of who we are. It's mutually beneficial. The company has a tangible presence in every city where we have offices.

- Corporate culture is a synonym for corporate personality. You have to ask yourself if you work best in a rigorous, buttoned-up, pressure-cooker atmosphere, or if your temperament is more suitable for a casual, idiosyncratic, foozball start-up? Fit between applicant and prospective company is a basic measuring stick of a successful interview. Find out about a company's culture before you interview there. Information about the culture is on a company's Web site. Another good resource is WetFeet.com.
- Observe the corporate culture while you are interviewing. What degree of formality does the interviewer use when talking to you for that hour? Do you go in an office and interview without interruption, (with the door closed and the cell phone on mute), or is the interviewer taking telephone

calls and leaving the room repeatedly for yet another "crisis intervention"? Do family photographs hang on the cubicle walls, or does the art consist of graphs and charts? Are people talking to one another in the hallways, or is everyone quietly focused on their work? There are a lot of cues around, so pay attention to them and try to determine whether you can see yourself working well in that environment.

- Look at the Corporate Values Page on a company Web site to determine the type of culture, but also consider the company's other offerings. Does the company have a friendly family leave policy? Does the company have a gym to promote fitness and health? Is the company active in the community? Does the company have an in-house learning program? Is the company committed to work/life balance? You need to understand a company's culture to answer the preceding question adequately.

- The cultural aspect you find most appealing also says a lot about who you are. If you chose to focus on the family-friendly policies, it tells the interviewer about your family priorities. If you chose to focus on the gym and the weekly basketball games, then an interviewer knows something about your values toward fitness and camaraderie. If you focused on the tuition reimbursement programs, then it tells the interviewer about your interest in personal development. These priorities may—or may not—fit in well with the company and the new position. That is up to you to find out. Knowing the ins and outs of the corporate culture is just as crucial as knowing what skills are required to do the new job—provided you want to make a good match. One Fortune 500 staffing manager said, "After passing the initial phase, hiring managers start thinking about fit."

13. Describe your "wow factor" to me.

Reply (Webmaster): This may sound odd, but functionality is a wow for me. If it doesn't work, I'm not interested in the fancy interface or flash design. It's all about easy navigation. Too many users are not completely competent when it comes to the Web. Times are changing, but we haven't arrived at full competency yet. One "clickisode"—that's what I call a mistake made by a user—and the buyer leaves the site before completing the purchase. I also like the fact that Web design allows me to use so many skills. I troubleshoot, create, publish—all in the name of a multimedia experience. I am lucky because I get to use my right brain/left brain: problem solving, decision making, creative, analytical. It's a great mix for someone who thinks as I do. Lots of Web designers are excellent at user interface and lousy at navigation. That's not going to work for me—or in e-commerce. You need to be able to capture data, persuade users to view a lot of pages, help them stick around for a while by allowing them to navigate easily and ultimately purchase something.

- Be yourself. Take a look at PSEG's definition of diversity: "Diversity is a value that is demonstrated through mutual respect and appreciation of the similarities and differences (such as age, culture, education, ethnicity, experience, gender, race, religion, sexual orientation, etc.) that make people unique." No one expects you to be a cookie-cutter version of the last employee who held the position, so don't pretend to be someone you aren't.
- Pause. Take some time to think about what you are going to say. An interview is not a race against the clock. It is better to be thorough and focused than to just blurt out anything because you haven't rehearsed an answer. According to Energy East's Lamoureux, "These [behavior-based questions] are hard to answer, so . . . the applicant should take his or her time."
- Define your vision. What makes you enthusiastic about the job you do each day? If "easy navigation" is a defining principle, then explain how that relates to your work as well as the work you hope to do. If streamlining procedures makes your brain cells bubble, then talk about how that wows you.
- Don't be afraid to tell the interviewer why you love your profession. Being engaged by your work is a prime component of job satisfaction. It's as much in the interest of the employer as it is in yours to ensure that the new job provides you with an outlet to feel satisfied, productive, and fulfilled.

14. Have you acquired a reputation for anything in your work?

Reply (Grant Writer): Yes, I am resourceful and I know how to build relationships with key players. It has a lot to do with my political savvy, but I am also known as an excellent project manager who can close deals in a timely manner. No detail is too small. If a contingency category holds up a transaction, it's important. In a recent $2.5 million deal, I recently acted as a liaison to several government agencies and a nonprofit organization. I created a business plan and grant to develop a for-profit business, which enabled low-income residents to gain full employment. I did this by searching and developing the potential funding resources. I then drafted an evaluation plan, prepared the documents for submission, rewrote the document to their specifications, and then followed through to ensure that the proposal met the guidelines. I never hide behind e-mail or avoid difficult situations. People should not have to spend hours on the telephone getting a minor detail resolved. That's why I set realistic expectations from the get-go, and I develop relationships with people who are not excessively bogged down in bureaucracy and inefficiency. Sometimes bringing all the parties concerned together is a gargantuan task, but I am known to be highly successful at brainstorming solutions for divergent groups. I have a lot of repeat business, which attests to the high level of satisfaction my clients have.

- This question can be intimidating at first, especially if you are a relative newcomer to your profession. Do not interpret the question too narrowly. This is not about superstar status. Think instead about what you were known for in your company or department, or even what you were known for in your internship. Pam Hill, a director of staffing and planning at Car-Max, said, "A candidate with lighter skills, qualifications, and experience [will] be considered [as long as] training time is available." For those who have not yet built up enough experience, think of this question as a variation of "What are your strengths and skills?" If you do have a reputation outside the company, though, then by all means elaborate.

- Sometimes strengths are not grand but instead quiet and subtle. Perhaps you lobby before the meeting to get attention for your agenda. Maybe you are always prepared at meetings so that when you articulate an idea, it is accepted and acted on. Maybe you try new presentation techniques to re-awaken an interest in a good idea recently ignored. To be an agent of change, you don't need the bright lights and hoopla. One Fortune 500 respondent said, "Most recruiters look at the candidate and decide if they like the candidate's personality—whether it will be a cultural fit. Cultural fit is probably key. Qualifications are important, but remember that a superstar in one company doesn't necessarily make a superstar in another company. At our company, we are not necessarily set up to fully support on-boarding every single person so he or she has some cushion—some bubble wrap around them so they don't blow themselves up. So it really is about the culture. We don't hire people who are high maintenance—personalities who think it is okay to throw a tantrum in the workplace."

- Your reputation begins to build as soon as you embark on a career. Every position you work in either solidifies your standing as a professional or detracts from it—regardless of the level at which you are working. Remember that industries are not as large and anonymous as you think. For good results, cultivate good relationships and "work hard for your money."

- Political savvy means learning to compromise, being flexible, and negotiating for results that satisfy divergent groups. You need others to get most things done, so learn to maneuver your way through a "political" landscape—whether it is in government, business, or even the classroom—and stop worrying about the negative connotations. Cast it instead in a positive light and think of political savvy as another term for the ability to build a consensus and get things done.

15. What competencies would you like us to help you develop?

Reply (Customer Service Account Executive): Actually, I would like to develop two areas. First, I would like to become more skilled technically. In my last position, I had many opportunities to use the new technology as well as teach it to customers—they called me the "bridge expert" because I could help anyone understand the basics—so I am very comfortable with technology. I noticed, however, on your Web site that for management associates you offer an opportunity to pursue a master of science degree in information systems that is available on-site through XX Institute. I would like to pursue that program. I am an advocate of lifelong learning, plus one of my strong points is discovering gaps in data. I see myself excelling in this program. Another way I would like to develop is by learning more management strategies. While at X Company, I was the youngest woman promoted to management in the North Jersey District, so I believe I have real potential. In the past, I have worked on teams and shown leadership qualities, but I still need better methods for getting others to jump on board an action plan. And my management skills need some improvement, especially in the area of conflict resolution. You have a lot of programs in place that I know I would take advantage of if I were given the opportunity.

- The preceding question gives you an opportunity to convince the employer that you are teachable, but first you need to recognize that there are, in fact, areas that need improvement. An honest appraisal of yourself is necessary to answer this question effectively.
- A level of competency must already exist before it can be developed, so don't express an interest in management training if, by nature, you prefer sitting in your office all day parsing data rather than interacting with peers and coworkers.
- Always balance your responses about "improvement" or "failure" or "obstacles" or "weaknesses" with positive attributes. A job interview is not the appropriate outlet for self-flagellation. Your confidence—or lack thereof—is very much a part of the evaluation process.

- Try to determine throughout the interview process if you are on the same page as the employer. Do you share the same values? Are you being honest with each other about the requirements and expectations for the job? Are you making yourself perfectly clear?
- Always know who the customer is for the particular company. Although some of the Fortune 500 companies surveyed are outwardly more customer focused than are others, all companies serve someone. Find out who that someone is and then articulate your understanding of the company's customer. At Alltel, Crane stated that, "many positions within Alltel are customer facing (both internal and external). If a candidate can't communicate clearly or would not be able to build relationships among different department members, then the demands of the position will not be met as easily."

16. What leader do you admire most and why? What have you learned from that person?

Reply (Account Manager): I just read *The Miracle of St. Anthony's* about Bob Hurley and his coaching tenure at St. Anthony's. I just finished coaching my daughter in basketball, and now she's moving up to the high school level, which is probably why I can relate to the book. Hurley coaches basketball at a small high school in Jersey City with 11 classrooms and fewer than 200 students. About 50 percent of the students come from homes that are below the poverty level. During his basketball coaching tenure, Hurley has had 800 victories, 22 states titles, and two national championships. The school doesn't even have a gym it can call its own. Hurley and two Felician nuns basically keep the school afloat financially—through a lot of positive public relations—because they get little funding from the church.

The book focuses on St. Anthony's undefeated 2003–2004 season, when Hurley had academically challenged and mainly dysfunctional kids. They were the toughest kids Hurley had ever coached.

Hurley accomplishes his goals by instilling discipline and having high expectations—regardless of the fact that a lot people would have looked at the numbers and written off these kids long ago. Hurley has gotten a lot of offers to coach elsewhere, but he's dedicated—and he knows he's effective in that environment. I admire this man's compassion, code of discipline and optimism, and standards of excellence. I am particularly impressed that in the last ten years, he has sent every one of his kids on to college—100 percent. In fact, in the 30 years that he has coached, only one student did not attend college.

Whenever my direct reports give me a hard time now, I tell myself that if Hurley can get his team to achieve—time and time again—then managing my group is really painless by comparison. I just have to keep my standards high, lead by example, and provide a specific framework in which my direct reports can achieve their objectives without microman-agement. My group is attuned now to what our primary purpose is.

- There are several ways to answer this question. You can choose someone who has inspired you, but don't pick Bill Clinton or George Bush unless you are absolutely certain that the interviewer shares your political affilia-tion (which would be difficult to determine under most circumstances). Choose someone less controversial. Another way to answer this question is to choose a role model in your community. This is a more parochial ap-proach, so be prepared to draw a full picture of this person's strengths, be-cause the interviewer will not have an understanding of who you are talking about without all the details. Another approach is to pick a historical fig-ure—someone who inspired you to move beyond your comfort zone; some-one who motivated you to stretch yourself. Do a little research before the interview on this figure.

- Make it as relevant to the new job as possible. The role model or leader you choose should have some qualities you aspire to. But you also need to have an understanding of how those qualities will be applicable at your new job. Staffing Director Suzann Snypp from BellSouth, a company with 60,000 employees, said when you go on a job interview you should "have a ratio-nale for why you are a good fit for the job and you should be confident of your own capabilities."

- No matter how unrelated the question may seem, make a connection to your work life. Even if interviewers ask you about your outside interests, they are primarily concerned about how you will function between the hours of 9 AM and 5 PM. Emphasize outside interests that will impact your work life; for instance, reading or golf or coaching sports teams or fund-raising for the local library.

- The preceding question (#16) is posed so the interviewer can get a sense of your values. As already mentioned, you need to think precisely what those values are—before the interview. Ask yourself if you subscribe to a strong work ethic? Do you favor team effort as opposed to individual effort? Do you admire high standards of excellence? Do you value creative freedom? What type of work environment suits you best? Do you favor a disciplined culture? Once you have thought about your work values, find the words to describe them. Jot your thoughts down on paper. Speak about them in a mock interview. Your communication skills are on display at a job interview. In fact, at CarMax, Pam Hill considers these skills to be a top priority: "Communication skills are universally more critical due to internal and external communication needs in most companies."

17. What have your accomplishments been in your current role?

Reply (Vice President/Sales): I am particularly proud of the fact that I was able to build a $600 million open-system business from scratch in five years. In addition—in fact simultaneously—I increased sales productivity 50 percent by generating more than 70 percent of this business from new accounts. Part of this success was due to the economic boom, but I also managed 2,000 people who were motivated to move wholeheartedly beyond the momentum.

I was also a member of the operations committee, which approved product directions, set marketing strategies, determined corporate expense plans, and partnered investment. This was the major steering committee at DGA, so its impact was profound and substantial.

And I successfully managed a budget in excess of $1 billion, which covered P&L, credit, technical support, account management, training, advertising, and promotion. Another accomplishment was the complete restructuring a few years back of field function to integrate VARs, OEMs, ISVs, telesales, teleservice, agents, subcontractors, integration channel partners, major accounts, and end users.

- You should know precisely what kind of impact you had at your former job so that you can quantify your results. Some jobs don't lend themselves as easily to this kind of quantification, but every job has varying levels of performance. Did you meet deadlines consistently? Did you reduce costs? Did you create new business? Did a piece of research that you unearthed help save the company millions? Did you improve standards? Did you exceed expectations? Are you adept at creating contingency plans? Did you motivate others to exceed their goals? And you can always emphasize your progressive responsibilities if quantifiable results are hard to calculate.
- Always expect follow-up questions. The interviewer will initiate what he or she wants to probe more deeply, but be prepared to offer additional information to back up the results you report. When you give an overview of

your accomplishments, be prepared to talk specifically about one or two points that are particularly relevant to the new job.

- If your most recent position was short term and you have absolutely no accomplishments to date, then reach back to the position that you held prior to your former position. Be prepared to explain, however, why you cannot elaborate further on your most current position.

- Try to determine what the employer values in the new position and emphasize those aspects of your current or former position that indicate you will fit into the new position well by solving the employer's immediate problems. Amy Moers Reeves, a director of corporate staffing at SYSCO, said, "Be prepared to give specific examples of experience you have that relates to the position and requirements noted in a posting."

18. What are your career aspirations, in both the short term and the long term?

Reply (Account Executive/Retail): I make resolutions every year, and I try to stick to them closely. Each year I review where I want to be the following year—both professionally and personally. So I have a one-year plan, but I also have a five-year plan. Professionally, my one-year plan is to spearhead international expansion. I have already increased my company's overseas market presence by 25 percent. I am especially interested in the new Chinese marketplace. I just came back from a trip to Beijing, and it was unlike anything I have ever seen before. It's an enormous emerging market, and I was so enthusiastic about the customer base that I even considered signing up for a language class in simple Chinese—even though I know fluency in this language would definitely fall into my five-year plan; maybe even my ten-year plan.

Just recently I teamed with other senior executives and played a key role in diversification of our product line by introducing new products to existing clients and marketing new brands to third parties. My one-year goal for sales growth of this line is 25 percent. I am almost there, and there are six months still left to the year. I intend to come as close to meeting these goals as possible, even if I am offered a position with your organization in the near future.

My long-term plan, five years from now, is to continue to work hard and advance, I hope, in your organization. As I already mentioned, I am particularly focused on the new market in China. I would welcome the opportunity to expand your presence there and become a pioneer, in a business sense, in that new marketplace. It's the fastest-growing economy in the world. Everywhere you turn you see construction cranes and stores overflowing with customers. Competition is fierce, but the retail market is finally opening up to foreign investors. I believe I could have a real impact in that arena. Some experts say high-margin sales in such a competitive market are pipe dreams, but that doesn't fall in line with my Beijing experience. So with the right opportunity and after five years, I expect to be the premier retail expert on the Chinese marketplace.

- Think ahead. Where do you see yourself professionally in one year? Five years? Ten years? Successful employees usually have a general idea of the direction in which they want to go—and sometimes even a specific plan. Ask yourself what steps you have to take to achieve your goals?
- Your expectations should be realistic. If you want to head up your own company, what stepping stones do you need to put in place so that you get to where you want to go. You want to convey yourself as a go-getter with a strategy to advance.
- Ambition is welcome in the marketplace, so you are allowed to have a vision or a dream, but don't suggest that you are willing to trample over others to achieve it. Try to check your ego at the door. Others will block your path if you come across as a brute. Brian Little, a group director of human resources at HSBC-North America, stated that "we look for results-oriented individuals who work well within teams."
- Be enthusiastic about your prospects. No dream is achieved without it.
- How much of yourself do you want to reveal to the interviewer? Just enough to show that you will be an excellent prospect—for the job for which you are interviewing. There's no need to tell the interviewer about your burning ambition to retreat to Tibet to join a colony of monks.

19. What influenced you to pursue a career in your particular area of expertise?

Reply (Paralegal): I have a bachelor's degree in history and am a diehard history buff, but I realized my career options once I graduated were limited unless I chose to teach, so I became a certified paralegal. Research and fact-gathering appeal to me more than teaching. When you study history, your main objective is to make sense of complicated situations by looking at cause and effect. The answers are not always evident, so you need to look closely at how one thing is related to another. Because I'm good at examining cause and effect, I asked myself in what field I could use this skill and earn a living. It seemed a natural fit to gravitate toward law. The law interests me—historically and otherwise—and working as a paralegal allows me to use the research, investigative, and writing skills I picked up as a history major.

I completed my paralegal certification at Kaplan while working on commercial litigation and litigation management in my current position at XX law firm. I work closely with the litigation attorneys, responding to interrogatories and other discovery requests. I am also adept at working with computerized databases, such as Lexis/Nexis. This work engages me because I am attuned by nature to sift through minutiae, and I am highly organized so I never lose track of supporting documentation. I have good writing skills, and the attorneys I work with at my current job appreciate my ability to state things clearly and in plain English. The attorneys have said again and again that I can find the story in the case. It saves them a ton of time as a result because I am able to whittle away unimportant details and get to the heart of the matter. Saving time is extremely cost effective.

I think my background in history and my subsequent training as a paralegal make me a good decision maker. I understand the complexity of events and the need to cull salient points from research.

- Always try to see how the question asked relates to what you did and want to do. Occasionally it is difficult to see the relationship, but you must remember you are on a job interview, so the employer is primarily interested in how you worked and how you will work in the future.
- Transferable skills are an important concept in the workplace. Every job has its own specifications—the variables differ for each position—so make a case that the transition will be smooth and efficient. Talk about the skills you have already acquired that will help you move easily into a position that may be different from the last one you held.
- Show the interviewer that you know what it takes to be successful in the job you are applying for and then weave that information into your responses as naturally as possible. Then convince the employer that you are a good match for the open position. According to Thrivent's Palmer, "While interviewing for a position, the candidate needs to prepare as if this is the only job he or she is interviewing for."
- Employers appreciate employees who increase profits or fix problems. Examine your past work history to see where you have been most effective. Maybe you assisted your supervisor in troubleshooting, or maybe you were part of a team that saved the corporation millions. Be prepared to talk about this.

20. Why is this position your next right move?

Reply (Media Planner): I actually think I am the right candidate for the job, but I am equally attracted to your company. I have worked in all mediums—television, print, guerilla marketing—so I know this background will be useful in your media marketing initiatives for national brands. Your media lab is a hotbed of creativity, and I would fit in perfectly there. I see enormous potential for growth in wireless, instant messaging, broadband, and gaming. I think your company is positioned best to take advantage of this opportunity.

I also like the work atmosphere here. You mentioned that brainstorming and team initiatives are the rule rather than the exception at X Company. This suits me just fine. My background suggests that I work best in a collaborative environment. The digital video documentary I worked on in 2004 required that I write, edit, produce, and even direct, but I had to work closely with a team of about ten other people to make this joint effort as successful as it was. I think I should mention that I can successfully operate on a shoestring and I am cost conscious, but I welcome the opportunity to work for a company that has the resources available to put the multimedia plan in motion.

- You are being interviewed primarily for a specific job, but emphasizing your desire to work at a particular company won't hurt your cause (unless you suggest inadvertently that you are not planning to stay in the offered position for a length of time).
- Companies "re-mine" applicants all the time, so stay thoroughly professional and upbeat no matter what. If you notice halfway through the questions that you are in way over your head—that the job is too much of a stretch for you—continue to do your best. Leave the interviewer with a good impression so that he or she will think of you in the future if a more suitable position opens up. No matter what the outcome, act like a professional. As one Fortune 500 participant said, "Always be alert to new opportunities."
- Say something. One- or two-word answers won't give the interviewer enough information to evaluate you. That's one reason why preparation is essential. Even if your communication skills are not as fine-tuned as you would like, research gives you something meaningful to say even if a tough question sneak attacks you.
- If your experience is very different from the requirements of the new job, try to reshape some of your experience so that it can be easily transferred

to the new position. Again, it's all about finding the connection between what you did and what you want to do.

21. Tell me about your qualifications and what experiences/skills you can bring to this organization that will add value?

Reply (Administrative Assistant): I have good skills overall, but I excel when a lot of detail is involved. I am an excellent proofreader. Reports that require a high degree of accuracy and technical knowledge showcase my talents well. I went to school at night to finish my associate degree, so I bring a high level of proficiency to my other responsibilities as well. I was continually chosen to develop and work on specialized safety reports and also highly protected risk reports that require accuracy and technical know-how. I am also adept at multitasking—simultaneously balancing scheduling and developing billing reports at the same time as providing customer service and resolving problems rapidly. My computer skills are more than up to speed. I am proficient in Word, Windows, Flow Chart, Excel, WordPerfect, and Lotus, and I am very good at Internet research. Customers have commented on my friendly and cordial manner on the telephone as well. I noticed that your job posting emphasized organizational skills. Well, my organizational skills are well tuned, so I can offer the kind of support that would be valued in a large company but also at a smaller organization, such as yours, where I have to wear many hats.

- If the job posting mentions particular computer software, mention either your proficiency or knowledge of that software. If you don't have even a bare minimum knowledge base, and you really want the job, then sign up at either your local library or community school for a crash course in the software. Alltel's Crane advised that "if you don't have a skill, get more training." Another Fortune 500 respondent said, "Show a willingness to go the extra mile."
- When you describe your skills overall to the hiring manager, make sure to put special emphasis on those skills that you would like to utilize in the new job. Many applicants are intuitive and can pick up on the signals of what is required at a new job—and then jump on board for the sake of getting an offer—but once they are hired, they realize the new job doesn't align itself with their expectations. Breakdowns in communication can occur as easily during a job interview as anywhere else, so strive to make yourself clear.
- Always think about how you can add value to the new company by having a positive impact on the bottom line. Can you streamline processes by get-

ting things done quickly? Can you implement best practices? Can you improve quality in products or services?

- Although computer know-how has nudged a good telephone manner to second place in the office, don't underestimate the importance of telephone skills. After face-to-face, it is the next-best tool for relationship building.

- Be proud of your achievements and don't compare yourself with others. Whatever course you took to get where you are today, honor it.

22. Why did you go to X college?

Reply (Engineering): Quite a few people have asked me that. College X is far away from my home base, but I thought that would be a good thing. I come from a small town and I think you tend to get a very narrow view of the world after spending 12 years in one school system. You begin to believe the world revolves around that small town. I always had an inkling that my hometown was not the center of the universe, so attending college 1,500 miles from there made complete sense.

Also, as you already mentioned, X College has an excellent program in engineering. The professors in that department are respected—and some even internationally renowned—throughout business and industry. I participated in the 3/2 engineering program, which allowed me to put off deciding the specific area of engineering to pursue until my fourth year of college. For three years I studied physics, which was a good option for me because initially I thought I wanted to be an electrical engineer, and as you can see, I ended up becoming a mechanical engineer—without any backtracking. The 3/2 program also gave me a broader background, which makes me more adaptable to this position than if I were highly specialized.

- Show the interviewer you can think on your feet or at least be objective about your situation. Pause if you must, but be responsive to the questions in a way that acknowledges the other person. You want to present the facts, but you also want to show your prowess on an interpersonal level. Prefacing your statements by referring back to what the other person has already told you draws the other person into the dialogue.

- Nearly every job has its own specifications, and employers want candidates who are highly teachable. Your educational background—the specific training and classes—is important but not as valued by employers as your ability to learn new processes, strategies, and systems. Degrees and certifications tell the employer that you are disciplined, teachable, and knowledgeable; however, they don't help the employer if you are rigid and all-knowing and can't learn the skills required to fulfill the specific position you are being offered.

- Follow the general-to-specific formula when answering questions. It puts your information into an easy-to-follow framework and balances the information well. You want to leave several openings for follow-up questions—whether they will be specific, hard-skill inquiries or more general, culture-fit queries.

- There is always a fine line between presenting yourself in a confident manner and excessive boasting (me-me-me). Give credit to others (for instance, the respected professors that got you where you are) for their expertise and impact on your life.

- Have a map for your future, especially if you are a recent graduate. Host Marriott's Lisa Whittington always asks candidates to list "three objectives for their development." Employers appreciate applicants who have mapped out a career path and have a commitment to lifelong learning. Know something about the direction where you want to go and provide specific stepping stones you plan to take to get there.

23. What is motivating you in considering another position?

Reply (Systems Analyst/Senior Manager): I have spent the last eight years at AB Company, and I feel as though I need more challenge and diversification. I am very good at what I do, but my primary responsibilities are not allowing me to grow sufficiently. I fulfill all the requirements of the job and even exceed expectations, but every time I lobby for a different role, I am told that I am doing such a great job as a senior manager in charge of the BARAMIS and AVPS systems that they don't want to rock the boat and upset everyone. I have been promoted from manager to senior manager, so I know they appreciate my efficiency and thoroughness and ability to get a job done, but I need to be challenged on a more regular basis. I have experience with all the development life cycles and many program management methodologies, and I would like to manage enterprise-wide programs.

- In many respects, this question is similar to "Why are you leaving Company X?" The only real difference is the word *motivate*, which implies that the hiring manager wants to delve deeper. What's more important to remember, however, is that this question surfaced in several disguises in the

Fortune 500 surveys, so you can be fairly certain that you will be asked why you are indeed leaving the company you are currently working for. Have a good answer.

- Of course the prospective employer knows that you are not completely satisfied with your current job, but you have to gingerly address this issue. Don't criticize your former employer and don't suggest that you are just an unhappy camper—no matter what the position. SYSCO's Reeves said this type of question often makes applicants uncomfortable. She added that "the reason why a candidate is looking or wanting to leave a position seems to cause some applicants to fluster."

- It is perfectly acceptable, however, to say that you want more challenge, more diversification, more avenues for advancement. These responses suggest that you have a reservoir of skills on tap for the next employer. You want to convey to the company what you have to offer it—not what it has for you. Just that slight switch in attitude makes you a more desirable candidate.

24. Explain to me a situation in which your business and personal ethics were challenged. Describe it and how did you respond to it?

Reply (Advertising Manager): That's a hard question. Let me think about it a minute. (Brief pause.) OK. I remember a situation a few years back. Post 9/11, the company was losing tons of money as were many others at that time. The CEO became a bear. After weeks of rumors, he told a group of his executives he was going to send around an e-mail to *everyone* in the company the following week announcing he would fire one person in each department. Morale was already bad because of the company's fiscal uncertainty—on top of the shock we were feeling about 9/11.

I knew who would be let go first in my department—the most recently hired ad exec. The problem was this ad exec had told me the day before that she was about to turn down an offer from a competitor. She was going to decline the offer as soon as the guy came back from his business trip. At first I tried to plant ideas in the ad exec's head that our competitor was a great company to work for and that she should get in touch and accept the offer. She wasn't convinced for a number of reasons but largely because of a childcare issue she had. This was not a large company, and everyone was on a first-name basis, so I went to the CEO and told him that if he was intent on sending out that e-mail and firing people in a few weeks, then he should just bite the bullet and get it over with because morale was already so low. I suggested he send out his e-mail immediately so we could move forward. I didn't want to betray the ad exec's confidence because I thought the CEO (in his delicate frame of mind) would turn around and fire the woman on the spot. The CEO sent the e-mail out the next day; the woman preempted her layoff and accepted the offer at the new company. I felt I handled that dilemma well.

- Ethical questions are difficult to answer at a job interview. They require some thought. So think of a situation beforehand. Think of how you were challenged. But when you think of a circumstance to describe, try to focus on an instance that will allow you to give an honest answer, preferably with a happy ending.
- So much emphasis has been put on conveying a positive attitude to the prospective employer. This does not mean that you present yourself as a Pollyanna. Unfortunate things happen, in business and in life, but you still need to portray a strong, can-do attitude even when the circumstances are gray or dark.
- Ethical questions are more open to interpretation than are other types of job interview questions. Rest assured, though, a thoughtful, honest answer will be better received than a facile half-truth. Applicants can become especially uncomfortable in an interview if they have been laid off or fired. One Fortune 500 participant said that whenever that topic arises, candidates should always handle it honestly, adding that "I've been downsized twice. I know what it's like." Alltel's Crane agreed, saying, "I realize that being laid off doesn't connote poor performance in all cases."

25. Describe your leadership style.

Reply (Financial Adviser): I have 18 years' experience at old-line companies, so I have managed large groups. I know how to create good outcomes primarily because I manage people well. First, I am an excellent communicator. I clearly state our goals and objectives to the group and delegate responsibilities. When I first started in my career, I had difficulty delegating. It had something to do with my ego. I thought no one could do it as well as I could. Then, after too many nights and weekend work and general burnout, I realized that it is more important to sacrifice a little perfection and instead get everyone involved. At the end of the day, the group accomplishes more than I ever could. On a recent global revenue plan, we had several new hires working on key sectors, so instead of reassigning the work to some already overburdened managers or doing it myself, I taught the new hires what they needed to know. They made a few mistakes, but we corrected it immediately, and it was a good experience for them. I like to teach now. I think it's important that the company is not so reliant on the expertise of one person. It makes the company stronger as well as the group.

Second, this took me longer to learn, but I now try to remain humble and validate others. Maturity has allowed me to not confiscate all the credit for a project's success. But I am accountable. I am a manager, so my group's success depends on how well I direct its efforts.

- When you are asked to speak about leadership, think emotional intelligence. Never portray yourself as someone who squashes others through sheer will. You might also want to refer back to the Lominger's core capabilities listed in Chapter 5.
- You probably won't be asked this question if you do not manage people, but that doesn't mean you don't have leadership potential. Think about how you like to be managed and expand on that. One Fortune 500 participant confessed that "for someone to fit in here, he or she needs to be . . . collaborative, definitely a good blend of left brain/right brain. So it's really key for [that person] to be emotionally intelligent. For the past couple of years, we are looking at our internal talent and grooming them."
- Think as well about good outcomes. Usually when a project is a success, it had something to do with a successful leadership style. Everyone has undertaken a project of one sort or the other. How did you achieve a successful outcome? How did you lead the way? Calmly, rationally, and step-by-step no doubt.
- Leadership inevitably comes back to relationship building. How do you empower others? Do you clear the path of obstacles so that others can move freely toward the objective? When you see yourself as the solution instead of the problem, you have the potential to lead.

9

YOUR QUESTIONS MATTER

*"My red flag is . . . inappropriate questions at the initial phase
of the interview, such as 'When can I take my first vacation day?'
or 'If I needed to call in sick, who do I call?'"*

DEB PALMER
Staffing Manager
Thrivent Financial for Lutherans

Once you answer the prospective employer's questions honestly and thoroughly, you get an opportunity to ask a few questions of your own. Ideally, your questions should grow organically from the Q&A that just unfolded. The interviewer has said something that piques your interest and you make a mental note. Usually, but not always, you have an opportunity to ask your questions at the end of the interview (after you have provided your answers). Occasionally, you get an opportunity to ask questions as you move along. Watch for cues from the interviewer. Usually a signal is obvious.

Today, unless you are applying for an internship or an entry-level position, you will probably meet with five to seven people before you are hired. Keep this in mind: you want to ask each of these individuals a few questions.

At Engelhard, where an applicant may meet up to ten people, Mangiarano said, "I ask them to let me get through my interview, and then I would be happy to respond to any questions they may have." If explicit directions on how the interview will be conducted are provided, then follow those directions to the letter.

Always have extra questions geared toward specific individuals or departments. Mangiarano explained: "I find it off-putting when candidates don't ask me questions because it tells me that they haven't done any homework on us or about the job. And when a candidate comes to me third or fourth in the process, and he or she says to me, 'Well, all my questions were already answered by the other interviewers,' I challenge them with, 'Well, I'm the head of HR; if you've got questions about our business, things that we do, people issues, career path opportunities, development opportunities, I'm the person to ask.' It surprises me that I give people the opportunity to ask questions and they decline."

Can you ever ask too many questions? Yes, according to HSBC's Brian Little: "A candidate should use the questions to show interest and, to a certain degree, to display their knowledge of the organization and position. Too many questions would indicate the candidate is unprepared." It's all about the *right* questions.

Throughout this chapter, sample interview questions are provided in the shaded boxes. These questions are specifically geared toward the various stages in the interview process. Generally, and depending on the size of the company, you'll meet or speak with a representative from human resources first (maybe through a telephone screen); then you'll meet with the hiring manager or be evaluated in a technical interview; then you may meet with some peers in the new department; and finally you may meet with the department head.

Each company has its own protocols, but it is fairly safe to assume that you will speak with *several* people from the new company before you are hired (either one-on-one or in a panel). Ask relevant questions based on the person to whom you are speaking and on the phase of the interview process. In other words, don't ask the HR generalist, "What are the most critical goals in the next three months for the department?" Save that question for the department head. Verizon's Thonis added, "We ask people to ask us questions because their questions tell us how they react and respond to us—and it's a sign of their mental vitality."

FILLING IN THE BLANKS

Some interviews are less structured. In other words, the interviewer expects you to ask questions as you move through the give-and-take. Career experts refer to this type of interview as conversational, but don't assume that *conversational* translates into casual. Every job interview is a *formal* process. Until you show up for your first day of work, refrain from assuming that you are on a first-name basis with anyone at the new company. In fact, even if the department head tells you to call him Andy during the interview, it would be inappropriate to send a follow-up thank you note with a salutation that reads "Dear Andy." Always err on the side of formality—even at an unruly start-up company with more than its fair share of independent and creative thinkers.

At Baxter International, a bioscience company that employs 48,000 people, Barbara Morris reported that interviewers at her company ask "standard questions" and also those that surface during "the discussion." This emphasizes, once again, that you must be responsive to the cues. If your interview more closely resembles a discussion, then expect some deviation from the standard Q&A format (in which the interviewer asks you a question, you respond, and then you're expected to move right on to the next Q&A). Depending on the rapport you have with the interviewer, he or she may give you several openings to jump right in and ask for additional information. In that case, the questions you ask should be organic—that is, pertinent—to the "discussion" you are having.

Fred Kavali, a retired engineer and businessman who recently donated $75 million to ten scientific research institutes, spoke about landing his first job in Los Angeles after getting off the boat from Norway in 1956. He didn't know much about sensors when he jumped on board the small company, but two years later he was able to start his own company. "In America, you don't have to know anything: you just have to ask the right question." He sold that company, Kavlico, for $340 million in 2000 and now spends a good part of his time endowing scientific research. As a matter of fact, three of the eight 2004 Nobel prizes for science went to scientists affiliated with Kavali's institutes.[1] Obviously, the questions matter.

Write down a list of questions that are organic to doing the new job. This should be part of your preparation for the interview, but don't memorize stock questions and answers. In an interview, you must be able to demonstrate that you can think on your feet. Mary Matatall, the director of global staffing at Continental Airlines, said interviewers at her company ask standard questions as well, but they are "behavioral-based questions based on the characteristics required" for the particular job. If you perceive an opening to ask your own questions during the Q&A segment of your interview, then make sure those questions are in response to the topic at hand. For instance, if the interviewer spends a considerable amount of time detailing the new e-mail marketing offering you would be responsible for, you may want to ask a specific question regarding whether you would be determining new methods or fine-tuning existing campaigns. An organic question—one that specifically relates to the information being exchanged—indicates that you understand the requirements of the new job.

So when you take a look at the sample questions, use them only at the appropriate interval, and don't just ask for the sake of asking. As Trang Gulian, a human resources manager at Fannie Mae, said, "Come prepared with well-thought-out questions, [but] have your listening hat on" as well.

The Q&A segment is the crux of every job interview. Standard questions are provided in the shaded boxes throughout Chapter 9, but it is a good idea to formulate your own in addition to these questions. Every job has its own specifications. Find out what the specifications are (as much as possible) ahead of time. If you don't know where to begin, parse the job description. Devote most of your preliminary research to preparing for the Q&A segment, but take a look at the information that follows also.

EXTENUATING CIRCUMSTANCES

Gray Areas

Title VII of the Civil Rights Act of 1964 prohibits employers from discriminating against candidates based on their sex, race, religion, age, or national origin. Even though this federal law has been in place since 1964, it still does not entirely prevent employers from asking illegal questions. If you are asked a question that suggests some form of subtle discrimination, do not react defensively by spouting off the telephone number of your lawyer. Occasionally these questions are asked by the interviewer in all innocence. Sometimes the questions are so well disguised that even interviewers don't recognize the illegal nature of their inquiries. Be tactful. If you don't feel comfortable answering the question, suggest that you don't think the interviewer's question is relevant to the requirements necessary to do the job. If the question is exceedingly discomfiting, then think twice about pursuing the job.

Then there are the questions that border on the illegal.[2] What constitutes an illegal question can vary from state to state. For instance, in one state it may be perfectly legal to ask you about your family obligations and in another state it's against the law. It is to your advantage to make your own inquiries about the laws in your state. Although no federal guidelines cover every illegal interview question, you may want to look at http://www.collegegrad.com/ezine/23illega.shtml, or the following article from the *Washington Post,* "38 Illegal, Sensitive, and Stupid Interview Questions . . . and How to Respond."[3] Reviewing this information should help you navigate through sensitive territory.

And what *is* sensitive territory? Anything that deals with age, alcohol or drug use, conviction record, citizenship, credit rating, disabilities, height or weight requirements, marital or family status, membership in an organization, military service, national origin, personal appearance, political affiliation, race or color, religion, sex, or union affiliation. Under certain circumstances, it is legal for employers to ask sensitive questions, but you should know the basics. Use the following link from Catholic University for more information about question guidelines: http://humanresources.cua.edu/manager/guidelines.cfm.[4]

Always keep in mind that a job interview is essentially a fact-finding mission—you are evaluating the company and the interviewers are evaluating you. For the match to be a success, the fit must work for both parties—even if the situation to find a new job is urgent. If your hot buttons get pressed too hard during an interview, then maybe it's not the right company for you.

Many career experts give applicants advice about circumventing illegal questions. Some even suggest that to avert age discrimination you should not list jobs on your résumé that go back more than 20 years. But think about it. Any company that resorts to these tactics is not a company you want to work for. Even if you got your foot in the door, this kind of environment won't be conducive to a good career experience. Steer clear instead. You are not desperate. Even if finding gainful employment is urgent, working for a company that is unethical is a stopgap measure. You will be doing yourself a favor in the long run to continue looking.

Questions to Ask about Development and Advancement

- If I take this position, is there room for advancement?
- What is the normal interval before someone in my position is considered for promotion?
- Do you assess employees' roles regularly?
- How do you develop people at this company?
- How do you help improve skills in teams?
- Do you provide cross-training?
- Do you provide cross-assignments?
- What kind of outside training opportunities (tuition reimbursement, training seminars, technical courses) do you provide to heighten skills and teach new knowledge?
- What happened to the person I am replacing? Was he or she promoted? Did he or she move to a different department? Did he or she leave the company?
- Is this company up-to-date on advanced training techniques to develop personnel?
- Can you tell me something about the corporate culture?

WORK GAPS IN YOUR RÉSUMÉ

As of this writing, more than 8 million people are still unemployed in the United States, according to the Bureau of Labor statistics. In fact, layoffs and early retirement packages are becoming the norm in some industries.

What do you do if you have to explain a work gap on your résumé? Much depends on the circumstances. The good news is that if you have been asked to come in for an interview, the employer is obviously interested in your explanation. Even though being laid off is traumatic, in today's world it's not that unusual. One Fortune 500 participant said two of the companies she worked for were downsized, and she even listed this information on her résumé.

Generally, the respondents to the Fortune 500 survey said that you should deal with a work gap—being laid off or fired or out of work for an extended period of time— as directly and honestly (and briefly) as possible. Everything comes out in the background check, so don't hedge or fudge. Fannie Mae's Gulian advised: "Provide enough details without sounding negative or bitter. Use the experience as a learning opportunity. Candidates should focus on adding value going forward, not backward." Host Marriott's Lisa Whittington said to keep your responses "short and to the point." Barry Martin of Timken suggested that applicants who have been fired from a previous job should provide only the most relevant details: "Only as much as requested by the interviewer. If the particulars are pertinent, the interviewer will ask for them and the candidate should supply them fully and openly." Alltel's Crane said, "I think the candidate should be honest. I understand personality differences and job fit can be contributing factors to whether or not a person is successful in a career. If the reason for being fired is not illegal, then they may still succeed in a position within our company."

As for sequencers, those who have made the decision to opt out of the work force to raise a family, the same advice applies. Dwell on the positive transferable skills you acquired while you were attending to other matters. SYSCO's Reeves stated that "it is perfectly acceptable to take time off or work part-time. Just tell the truth." Often while raising a family, individuals become involved in volunteer work or less demanding positions. Lamoureux, a director of human resources planning at Energy East, said: "People are always worried about providing an honest answer to why there is a gap in their employment if it's related to their family . . . That being said, it would be helpful for candidates to demonstrate how they kept their skills up-to-date during the time they were off, especially because business is changing so quickly."

KEEPING YOUR SKILLS POLISHED

Several references have been made throughout this book to the importance of keeping your skills fresh and up-to-date. By all means, take community school courses, enroll in certification classes and investigate development programs. Many programs are inexpensive or even free. The Gateway Workforce Development Program, a Bronx-based employment services organization partnered with Columbia University, selects 20 candidates to attend class once a week at the computer lab at the university to obtain "on-the-job" experience by being put in a "real working condition." Other state and local organizations offer similar programs.

If you are currently raising a family or taking care of a disabled or elderly family member, commit yourself to keeping your marketable skills current. Plan ahead; investigate the programs in your area and sign up for a class as soon as possible. Although courses about gourmet cooking and Zen meditation may be good for the soul, it is especially important that you keep your computer skills current. The digital age is in full swing, and the technology changes so quickly that you may need annual—or even semiannual—brush-up courses just to keep pace.[5]

VOLUNTEER EXPERIENCE

Emphasizing your volunteer experience also applies to newcomers to the work force. In "Doing Well in Your Career by Doing Good Outside It," Eilene Zimmerman wrote this: "Human resource professionals say volunteer experience is invaluable to recent graduates without experience in their chosen fields" because volunteer experience tells the employer several things.[6]

- You are an active, enthusiastic, and involved member of your community—attributes that will invariably be carried over to the workplace.
- You undoubtedly picked up transferable skills that can be applied to your new job. Maybe you were a coach; maybe you were a teacher; maybe you were a fundraiser; maybe you made Free/Open Source contributions. All of these activities suggest that you have not spent the last three months (or three years) on the couch eating chips.
- You care about others so, according to Zimmerman, "you can be trusted."

INTERNSHIPS

Student internships, too, are invaluable in providing marketable skills. In fact, these programs are so ubiquitous now that you may have to explain to a prospective employer why you did *not* participate in an internship during your college tenure. Even if the internship is only remotely connected to the new job, it is still valuable because of the real-world exposure it gives a newcomer. Because working in an office can be a shock to the system, employers prefer that you work out these kinks in an internship.

Most internship interviews, however, deviate from the standard job interview. For one thing, the emphasis is primarily on gaining experience, so:

- You will not negotiate salary (some internships may provide a stipend).
- The position is temporary (unless you are hired after you graduate).
- Most internships are arranged in the career office at the college or university, but occasionally internships are found independently. Career offices still arrange the college credit, so don't delay in notifying them. It is a good idea, in fact, to investigate the procedure for internships ahead of time (some colleges and universities require prerequisites before embarking on an internship).
- Instead of meeting with three or four individuals at the prospective company, you may meet with only one person and be invited to participate based on a brief interview (15 minutes is not unusual).
- The first impression is crucial. (Can you make the transition to the professional world with ease?) In other words, treat the interview process formally by dressing neatly, communicating clearly, and following up with a thank you note, but it is unlikely that you will be grilled about your qualifications and skills (as you basically don't have much experience).

CAREER CHANGE OR ALTERATION

Then again you may have reached a point in your life where you want to change things dramatically by embarking on a whole new career. A new direction obviously takes more planning, but the strategy remains the same. Find the company or organization or even your own business or profession that is a good match for the new you. Then develop the skills needed to enter and flourish.

An excellent book for those considering a new profession is Richard Bolles's classic *What Color Is Your Parachute? A Practical Manual for Job-Hunters and Career-Changers.*[7] According to Bolles, the key to understanding and implementing a career change is the "vision"—"the picture of *the life you really want* that you need to be concentrating on. It has the power to bring about the very change you desire."

Career changes usually begin by easing into the new business on a part-time, volunteer, or entry-level basis. For instance, if you want to open a B&B, offer to be a short-order cook at a successful B&B in a nearby town. If you want to fulfill your lifelong aspiration of becoming a painter or a playwright, volunteer at a gallery or a community theater. A second career can be as demanding as the first. Just speak to the dentist who becomes a biology teacher in his mid-50s. A new career or starting a new business can often translate into 60-hour work weeks. But at least you will love what you're doing—and that's the whole idea.

For certain experienced workers, changes may resemble only slight adjustments. Some older workers won't be changing careers but rather realigning themselves from key players to mentors. This type of realignment is about to move into the spotlight. According to *Fortune*'s Anne Fisher, "By forcing out the employees with the most experience, companies may be inadvertently pushing critical knowledge out the door before it is shared with the next generation."[8] To battle this brain drain, several large corporations are providing incentives to older workers to stay put a little longer so they can transfer knowledge to Generation X employees. New rules being considered by the Treasury Department and IRS may sweeten the plan. If the rules are passed in 2006, older workers will be allowed to phase their way out of the workforce while still continuing "to accrue pension benefits despite working fewer hours, and their smaller paychecks wouldn't affect the formula for determining final benefits."

What does this have to do with job interviews? First, if you are an older worker, then leverage your experience to the maximum. Join a group of like-minded professionals and become a resource for companies that will need to tap into the knowledge base of more experienced workers as the baby boom generation retires "in droves." According to Fisher, "GE's Bob Corcoran . . . envisions a future, not far away, in which 'people aged 65 to 80 will share a job with someone else or work "core hours," 10 to 3, or work part-time and take extended leaves to share their expertise with nonprofits.'"

Second, "shadowing" will take on a whole new meaning—and not just for interns or newcomers to the job market. Acquiring knowledge from mentors and more experienced workers will become a premium skill in and of itself. By becoming the new repository of knowledge, your value to an employer will increase tenfold.

Companies are aiming recruitment efforts at the older workforce for lower-paying jobs as well. In "More Help Wanted," Milt Freudenheim wrote that MetLife, Pitney Bowes, Borders, Home Depot, Principal Financial, Wal-Mart, and Walgreens are actively seeking older workers to fill a variety of positions. "For one thing, the older workers are much less likely to depart after a few years. The turnover rate for employees 50 and older was one-tenth that of workers under 30."[9] Some companies even have "snow-bird" specials, whereby an employee can work at one branch or store in a northern area during the milder months and then at a southern branch or store during the winter months.

The hiring landscape has changed—but so has the workforce. According to Freudenheim, "At Pitney Bowes, a manufacturing company that is also big in business services, almost 1 in 4 employees is over 50." The workplace and workforce are indeed in a state of transition. Why not position yourself so that you can take advantage of the opportunities? It's all about remaining flexible and open. And don't forget to reach for the stars—no matter what your age.

Spend time on the Internet, take some classes, travel, volunteer, and explore all your options. Bolles stated, "The disadvantage of the life-changing job hunt, of course, is that it is not quick, it requires quite a bit of effort and it requires a maximum of thinking." The good news is now that you are a seasoned professional—mature and wise—priorities become easier to identify, and with a little creativity, who knows! The second stage of your life may turn out to be more rewarding than the first.

Questions to Ask about Your Management Role

- Will I have an opportunity to be trained or debriefed by my predecessor?
- Who are the key stakeholders (customers, senior management, peers) who can affect my success or failure?
- Will I be able to read past performance reviews of the people in the group I am going to manage?
- How does this group keep metrics of its success?
- Is there someone in particular I should speak to regarding the department's consulting services?
- How would you rate the capabilities of the staff I am going to manage?
- Can you identify the steps I must take to maximize my success as a leader of this group?
- If the group had a personality, how would you describe it?
- Does the group normally meet its deadlines?
- Can you describe the projects in which the group had trouble overcoming obstacles?
- What were the specific obstacles?
- Can you describe some of the projects at which the group excels?

TANGIBLE EVIDENCE

Everyone loves a visual—and hiring managers are no exception. You might think this idea is suitable for graphic designers and other creative artists, but how does it pertain to someone applying for a position in finance? It's a broader category than you think. Samples—or visuals—tell a story to an employer that your words may not. Anita Bruzzese, a syndicated career columnist for Gannett, said in an interview, "This is why it's so important that you have the records of kudos from a boss or a memo from a team leader saying, 'We couldn't have done it without you.' All those things you need copies of, so that you can actually show your value to an organization."

Energy East's Lamoureux also stressed the importance of having samples of your work. She said a sample lends "concreteness to the interview." So if you worked on a brochure or a training program or even sample code, put together a neat folder or binder that highlights your work and bring it to the interview. Just make sure that whatever you show the prospective employer is not proprietary information.

Fannie Mae's Gulian also suggests that returnees to the workforce especially should "show examples of any activities or training that they were involved in during the break." For instance, if you were involved in fundraising for your local library or you put together a recreation program for children, create a folder with news articles that mention your name or accolades that you received as a result of your leadership or participation.

Samples like these provide the solid evidence a hiring manager may need to make a decision in your favor. When you put together your own version of a portfolio, it displays a professional approach toward your work and other interests—it tells an employer you are serious about the interview process as well as the prospective company.

Questions to **A**sk about the **D**epartment

- What are the most critical goals for this department in the next year?
- Who is the primary client/customer for the services of this department?
- What problems do you anticipate I will face in my new role?
- Will I be expected to work on existing campaigns, or will I be expected to create appropriate change when the time comes?
- If you could use one word to describe this department, what would it be?
- What are some of the unwritten rules of working in this department?
- Could you describe a typical day in this department?
- On a scale of 1 to 10, how important is teamwork in this department?
- Do you expect this department to grow in size and scope within the next year or two?

FINISHING TOUCHES

The Fortune 500 survey participants were asked about following up interviews with thank you notes. A perfect score (100 percent) said they never disqualified a candidate because he or she didn't send a thank you note. TIAA-CREF's Moll said, "Excellent candidates are too hard to find to set up an administrative task as a benchmark. But a [thank you note] is a plus." On the other hand, Office Depot's Anne Foote Collins acknowledged that even though she has never personally disqualified a candidate because of this, "I know of hiring managers at other companies who have." So the message is clear: send a thank you note after your job interview.

In an "Ask Annie" column in *Fortune,* Fisher recommended that you send a thank you note to each individual you met with at your interview—even if that means eight people.[10] Send a brief (four or five lines) note—"handwritten, sent via snail mail"— that is a "little different, including something that you discussed" in each meeting. If there is any issue that needs more extensive coverage than a few lines, then type the letter but still send it snail mail. Keep it simple: Showing an employer your gratitude with everything from hand-delivered notes to gimmicky displays should be avoided because you are a professional and you don't want to appear desperate.

PAY ATTENTION TO THE TIME FRAME

Every Fortune 500 respondent said he or she expected applicants to ask questions. How many depends on the level of the job and the rapport with the interviewer; however, be aware that most interviews last approximately an hour, especially if you are interviewing with a representative of human resources, where the interview is more structured than it is when you meet with a hiring manager or peers in the department. Thrivent's Palmer recommended that "the first thing a candidate needs to verify is the amount of time . . . permitted for questions. If . . . a specific amount of time . . . can be allotted to questions, [candidates] should ensure they do not run over that time limit."

That's one of the reasons to keep your questions focused on the areas of particular interest to you. You probably won't have an opportunity to have *all* of your questions answered initially, so pace yourself. Be considerate of the interviewer's time, and don't be tempted to pose a throwaway question just for the sake of asking. Aim for a concise and equal exchange of information. Jabil Circuit's Otto agreed: "We encourage our candidates to ask questions and interview us just as much as we are interviewing them to see if it is a fit for both parties concerned."

Q u e s t i o n s t o A s k a b o u t Y o u r F u t u r e B o s s

- How many direct reports are you responsible for?
- You have a lot of responsibility. How accessible are you to those you manage?
- How is conflict managed in the department? Do you resolve it or do you expect the team to manage themselves?
- How often will you informally assess my performance?
- How do you help improve the skills of the team?
- What committees exist within the department?
- Do you have your own personal board of directors (a core group helping you make decisions that impact the group)?
- What types of measurement systems do you have in place within the department?
- What are the department's short-term and long-term goals?
- Are there any organizational obstacles that may impede you from achieving your objectives within the department?
- What are two major goals I will be expected to achieve this year?
- How do you see me fitting into the department?
- I just want to make sure I understand everything, and we are all on the same page. Can you give me an idea of what you see me doing on a day-to-day basis?

10

THE OFFER

"We provide a general salary range during the first round of interviews and give specifics at the offer."

SHERRI MARTIN
Director of Human Resources
Deere & Company

The match has been made and the new job fits you like your favorite pair of jeans. All the signals are there that you are the answer to the company's dilemma. The exchange of information has satisfied both parties—the interview was a success! You want the new job and the employer wants you.

Chapter 5 refers to the "reward values" listed in *Maximum Success,*[1] so before you sit down to contemplate the company's offer, consider what really motivates you. For some, money may be the primary drive; for others, it's a flexible schedule; for many, it's engaging work. Decide what's important to you and then be prepared to do . . . more research.

When you first started the process, you got a general idea of what the salary range was for someone in your profession. That information is easy to find just by investigating various Web sites for salary ranges or going to career centers[2, 3] or speaking to other professionals in your field. But now you have a specific offer in a specific town with a specific company—and it's time to crunch the numbers and do the math.

NEGOTIATING A SALARY

The topic of salary comes up at varying points in the interview process at Fortune 500 companies. The important thing to remember is *not to mention salary until the discussion is initiated by the interviewer.* "Until salary is brought up, don't talk money," said Ted Horton, a managing partner with BCI Partners (a private equity investment firm).

Some of you will balk.

OK, balk, but keep it to yourself. You cannot truly negotiate anything until the topic arises. Be patient instead. You may knock yourself out of the running by demanding something the company is not yet ready to give, and protocol differs at each company. Some employers request that you state your salary range in your cover letter; some employers get a feel for the range in the telephone screen or first interview, and others wait until the final stages of the interview process—until they are absolutely certain that they want you on board—before they even mention dollars and cents.

You can do several things while you're waiting for the offer. First, consider several variables. Do you have to relocate (that's a negotiable item)? Do you have a particularly long commute (travel costs should be factored into your base)? Do you warrant top-of-the-range pay (your résumé is full of accomplishments and exceeded goals)? Will you be working for a big company (with predetermined salary ranges) or a small company (where salary may be more flexible)? Do you have generous benefits (that's something worth negotiating as well)? Do you expect a signing bonus (ask if that's part of the deal)?

Anita Bruzzese, syndicated career columnist and author, advised that "when you are negotiating salary for a new job, that's always the best time to get the salary you need. If you say, 'Well, I'll wait until I get my foot in the door, and then I'll ask for X number of dollars,' it doesn't work that way. What you get on your first day of work is the best time to get what you are worth. You need a good starting point." BCI Partner's Horton added this: "Candidates should always go in high. Big companies may have ranges, but smaller companies usually do not. At small companies, there are no hard and fast rules. It's all a function of where you begin. So the higher the starting salary, the better off you're going to be going forward. It's the only time you really have the leverage."

TIMING IS EVERYTHING

Some companies request that you state your salary requirements immediately, in fact, in a cover letter. Ideally, you wrote in your cover letter that your salary was either "negotiable" or "competitive"—and you did not give a specific figure or range. It's normally not a good sign when a company asks for your salary requirements from the onset, because companies are basically doing one of three things: (1) eliminating candidates from the applicant pool based on salary;

(2) determining what a phantom job is currently worth; or (3) revealing that the right price (rather than the right candidate) is its number one concern. If you did put figures in your cover letter, preferably you gave a range that was wide enough to accommodate your needs ($50,000 to $60,000) but not so wide to render it meaningless ($55,000 to $95,000).

The same advice goes for salary history. Some companies ask for this information up front—in the cover letter or employment application. Trying to predetermine salary before the company gets to knows you and you get to know the company is a fuzzy science at best. Avoid stating your salary history if at all possible. On the employment application that asks for a salary history, Nick Corcodilos suggests that you write "confidential"; and in your cover letter, write "to be discussed at interview."[4] Cocodilos added: "When you provide your salary history, you give up your negotiating leverage." Remember, though, some background checks reveal salary data.

You could avoid this pigeonhole by neglecting to state your salary history altogether, but then you may risk losing the opportunity to interview (unless, of course, your professional accomplishments are so outstanding that the company decides to bring you in face-to-face, even though you neglected to provide the information it requested). What's important to remember is that if a company insists on a salary history, then negotiating more than a 10 or 15 percent increase in salary at your new job is going to be next to impossible.

If you decide to provide a detailed salary history before the interview, then put the information in a separate document (other than your cover letter or résumé).[5] Make sure you state the starting as well as the ending salary to show your progression. Including some of the perks that went along with your current or former position, such as your 401(k) and vacation time, is also advisable. Companies that stipulate salary histories, however, are usually less flexible when negotiating it in the final stages. If you expect a significant boost to your salary in your next position, then you may want to avoid applying for positions with companies that consider salary the number one benchmark.

Going back to patience, avoid a discussion of salary for as long as possible. You put yourself in the best negotiating posture after you have *sold your interest* in the company based on who you are and what you have to offer. You have a much better chance of winning what you need when the employer is eager to have you on board. But remember, the best time to negotiate—always—is when an offer is made. Why?

Because at the initial stage of the job search, you are merely an anonymous entity (especially at the résumé and cover-letter stage), so the less said the better. Midway through the process, there are still many viable candidates. By the end of the process, the choices have narrowed, and you have managed to persuade the employer that you are the perfect fit for the job and the company. The chemistry is in place. Finally, it goes back to what Engelhard's Mangiarano declared earlier: "You never can negotiate anything that's not offered. To talk about salary with a candidate at an interview is inappropriate until an offer is made."

It is your responsibility then to find out how the negotiation *process* begins or unfolds at the prospective company. If your best friend told you about the open position, probe further about the negotiation process (rather than about specific numbers). If a headhunter gave you the lead, ask the headhunter for full details about the stage at which you can expect this conversation to begin. If a salary base or range was posted on the company Web site, keep your antenna up when speaking to the interviewer to detect when this topic becomes relevant. At Engelhard, Mangiarano said that "what I do is tell a searcher what my target salary is, what my range is, what incentives or perquisites, if any, apply. And for somebody to come in and discuss that with me after he or she has been told all that information by a searcher is, in my judgment, quite bad taste because it's about the job and the fit. You have the opportunity to market yourself to me. And then it's about the opportunity for me to market the company to you. And until such time when we decide that we want to dance together, there's no real reason to put on the music."

Because recruiting software is dramatically altering the hiring landscape, your first contact with a prospective employer may be through the company's recruiting software on a company's Web site. If you apply electronically using the company's recruiting software, a salary base or range may be posted, but the figure is more a guideline, and negotiation is still an option. Kevin Marasco, director of marketing at Recruitmax Software, said, "Our customers [the employers] typically utilize salary ranges (low/mid/high or low/high), leaving room for negotiation based on perceived value, experience, and so on. This information is typically displayed only internally, although they do have the option to show the candidate (rarely done, and a broad range when it is posted). Most customers also use an offer-approval process, where once an offer is extended, it has to be approved (as defined in the system's configuration but typically by a hierarchy of managers) before going to the applicant. Candidates can also accept/reject/negotiate the offer online (via the career site or e-mail)."

Whatever you do, to get the best offer you must follow the company's protocol. You should also keep your head clear of any emotional baggage that you may have in regard to money. Stay rational and centered instead. You can shortchange yourself if you don't remain calm at all times. For those who are uncomfortable with the dollars and cents aspect of the interview, rest assured that everyone knows you are a complex, multifaceted individual. The job interview, however, is an appropriate juncture to place a dollar value on your contribution, so don't be timid. Get all your facts in order—and let go of the feelings—for the best possible outcome.

BCI Partner's Horton said that protocols differ, depending on the size of the company. "Again, are you going to General Motors or are you going to a private company that might only have 20 or 30 employees? You have got to know where your latitude points are. Who is more flexible? General Motors or IBM probably has everything labeled and tracked, so you probably are not going to have much latitude. But if it's a partnership or private company, I think you do have more latitude, and I think you can be a little more creative on your way in the door."

THE NUMBERS SCREEN

Many Fortune 500 hiring professionals said that a salary range is "probed" in the initial telephone screen—just to make sure the applicant and the company are in the same ballpark. Thrivent's Palmer stated that the topic of salary is first mentioned "during the phone screening. We confirm a rough salary range the candidate is expecting to ensure we are in a negotiable range with the candidate. At the first interview a more formal conversation regarding salary expectations (base and bonus) is confirmed."

Most Fortune 500 companies have salary ranges for particular jobs, so you will usually be negotiating within that framework. You should have a *range* too—before you even show up for an interview. Make sure, however, you don't get hung up on a specific number ("I want $68,000 or else"). Instead, stay flexible in the event that your dream job presents itself. Think *range*—and keep it reasonable.

Even if you must discuss a range during a telephone screen, Bruzzese suggests that you stall as long as possible before committing to specific numbers: "What you want to do is you want to say, 'In my mind, it's too early to talk about salary. I would much rather discuss my skills in XYZ area. I see what you're saying here, but let me tell you about the time I saved my company $5 million because I caught an error . . .'"

On the other hand, if the hiring manager is required to pin you down at this stage, make sure you are comfortable with the figures. There is no point telling yourself that you'll get the employer to jump up a hefty notch once he or she falls in love with you. If the hiring manager is determined to nail you down in the phone screen, then the likelihood of boosting the offer to a much bigger paycheck at a later stage may be nothing more than a pipe dream. Then you have to ask yourself, why waste your time or the employer's time? If the figures don't work for you at this stage, they won't work for you when you show up for your first day of work either—unless you sell your house and your car and farm your children out to their grandparents.

But if the salary range discussed during the phone screen is slightly below expectations but not fiscally impossible, pause. Gently steer the conversation away from money for a moment and consider what it is you really want from your new job. Whatever you do, don't throw away the opportunity to interview just yet. Jeanne Sahadi, CNN *Money* writer, advised that "another component to your compensation" is your "psychic income. Put simply, it's whatever rewards you derive from your job that can't be neatly quantified by a dollar sign. And those rewards can be just as important as a paycheck, although one without the other is like Abbott without Costello."[6]

NEWCOMERS TO THE JOB MARKET

When you don't have a lot of experience under your belt, salary requirements get tricky because you can't base your new salary on what you were earning at your last job and you usually are short on the career accomplishments you need to leverage a better salary. That's why it is essential to spend a considerable amount of time researching what the starting salary is for someone in your field. An excellent resource for current salary guidelines is a college career services department (make sure to look at the quarterly National Association of Colleges & Employers [NACE] Salary Survey). The U.S. Bureau of Labor Statistics (BLS) Web site also has salary information.[7] The BLS site is comprehensive and may take hours to explore, but the information is useful. Another useful Web site for newcomers who are determining their worth in the marketplace is the *Wall Street Journal* site.[8]

Also make sure to factor in your location. For instance, you need to earn considerably more if you plan to live in the San Francisco Bay area than you would to live in Orlando. Take a look at http://www.salary.com and plug in the relevant information into its Cost-of-Living Wizard—a calculator that compares "living-cost indexes and salary differentials." Take notes. Then when you get an offer, you can counter in an informed and reasonable manner—based on the facts.

In addition, if your skills are particularly marketable—maybe you participated in several internships or you spent your evenings working in the college's computer lab—then factor those skills into the equation as well. All newcomers to the job market are not equal in terms of skills, so be realistic but don't shortchange yourself.

"You must show the employer how your participation led to success," Bruzzese said. That piece of advice applies to your college career, your part-time job, your internship, your fundraising for your sorority, or your role as a point guard on the basketball team. At an interview with Office Depot's Anne Foote Collins, the recruiting director gives newcomers an excellent opportunity to speak to this success: "I ask about their college experience: why they selected the college they went to and their major. I find it's a question that puts them at ease and it's a fun way to start an interview." This type of question provides you with an opening to differentiate yourself from the competition—and maybe even boost your starting salary.

Finally, decide what's most important to you at your new job. Perhaps the new company is a draw because you would be working with outstanding professionals who are capable of teaching you the ins and outs of the business. Maybe the opportunity to travel is attractive, or possibly the development, training, and education the new company provides are a priority. Whatever appeals to you, weigh all those advantages. Then negotiate the best salary you can, so you don't have to spend the next five years climbing out of a deficit because you initially undervalued yourself.

One last note to newcomers: when you negotiate salary with an HR professional, remember it's comparable to talking about last night's game with a TV sportscaster. HR professionals know the salary ropes, so make sure you have all the facts to justify your requirements. Good negotiators respect worthy opponents. Those skills you learned on the debating team while you were in high school? Use them.

THE FIRST FACE-TO-FACE

If the topic of salary doesn't come up until your first interview, it means you are getting closer but not especially in the ideal position. Several Fortune 500 respondents talked about the process at their company: Allied's O'Leary said, "HR will usually bring up [this topic] in the first interview upon review of salary requirements listed on the required application." Jabil's Otto said she also discusses salary at the first interview: "The candidate is asked up front 'What is your acceptable salary range?' The purpose of this is to ensure that the candidate knows our salary range and also we get a better understanding if he or she is going to fit within the range. We have a very thorough but relatively quick turnaround process from the time the candidate interviews until the time an offer is extended/declined." PSEG also has a quick turnaround process. Garofalo reported that "so far this year, we have been averaging about 40 days" (instead of the average three to six months). But Garofalo added, "Salary is predetermined for bargaining-unit positions. For nonunion positions, it is considered when the hiring manager wishes to proceed with the offer." At HSBC-North America, Little said the topic of salary comes up "during the first interview. We don't want to waste anyone's time. Many applicants don't want to discuss salary, but we have found it saves time and money to be clear about expectations from the very beginning."

Whether a specific figure or a range is discussed, do everything in your power to keep the discussion open ended. This doesn't mean you don't answer the interviewer's questions. But instead of committing to specifics, say, "Yes, I will consider that salary if . . .

- the work engages me because it is varied and challenging.
- the supervisor and my peers are people I can work well with.
- the company provides many training and/or development opportunities.
- the company provides room for advancement.
- the working conditions are amenable.
- the company is secure and diverse.

Fill in the blanks after *if*. It's going to be different for everyone. Perhaps on-site day care or a flexible schedule tops your list. Perhaps the reputation of the new company matches your needs for affiliation. Perhaps earning potential is your bottom line. You have to know ahead of time exactly what factors are important. Naturally you are in a better position to talk about your salary after you have gone through all the rounds of the interview, but keep these things in mind when the topic of salary surfaces in your first interview. Remember you are motivated to remain open, flexible, and reasonable because your former or current position has given you the impetus to make some necessary changes.

- *Your new supervisor.* You have pondered what it will be like to work for a new supervisor. Your spirits are lifting already. In other words, no more *agita* from your former boss.
- *Your new job.* The work you will be performing at your new job seems challenging and will have an impact on the organization. The mind-numbing busywork of your former job will be merely a memory.
- *Your new coworkers.* Everyone seems to be on a first-name basis, and your new peers seem friendly, helpful, and engaged by their work. Your nemesis in accounting . . . gone.
- *Your new company.* The new company is growing and there's room for advancement. A refreshing change of pace from the last place you worked, where the only strategy management could come up with for generating income was periodic layoffs.

THE DOLLAR VALUE

Skilled negotiators have all the facts at their disposal. In this book's predecessor, *Get the Interview Every Time,* a term that repeatedly surfaced in the Fortune 500 survey and formed the basis of that book was *return on investment* (*ROI*).[9] Job seekers who were scooped up quickly by prospective employers were those who could demonstrate quantifiably that they produced good results at their former or current jobs—either by increasing profit or eliminating problems. In fact, many companies aggressively seek out high-performing candidates and may at times "poach" employees from their current jobs—what Recruitmax's Marasco calls the "passive candidate." Building a reputation as an excellent employee—someone with considerable ROI—often makes the journey to a new job softer and gentler.

You may be saying to yourself that because you work in the law firm's library, it's difficult to quantify your contribution. Bruzzese said you may have to rethink that appraisal. According to her, ". . . I always suggest when you go into any kind of interview that you can recite chapter and verse the things you contributed to. 'I worked on a $5 million-dollar project and my contribution was XYZ. They would not have found this obscure piece of research if it had not been for my searching for it.' Everybody plays a part."

In Chapter 8 you got a sample of the questions Fortune 500 hiring professionals asked applicants. Some are standard questions, some are thought provoking, and some are complex and difficult to answer. The theme that should pull all those questions together for you is that your contribution at work must be a facet of all the answers to those questions. This goes for the salary-negotiating process as well. Knowing the exact nature of your contribution will make the company's offer that much stronger.

Bruzzese continued, "You wouldn't be an employee if you did not play a part. If you're going to sit there and warm your chair, you're not going to last very long. Maybe you're not the project manager, but if you were on a successful team, then know what your role was and speak about it confidently." Assert yourself, in fact. Tell the company about the ROI it will see as a result of giving you the salary you are asking for. After a calm and reasonable negotiation, the company will usually return the favor.

THE MIND SET OF NEGOTIATION

Negotiation is a skill that you may not yet possess. If you haven't done so already, educate yourself quickly before the next salary discussion. Watershed Associates, a company that offers consultative negotiating training worldwide, has a recommended reading list for those interested in sharpening their skills. You might want to take a look at www.watershedassociates.com for further information. Ruth Shlossman, a director at Watershed and frequent speaker, offered advice during a recent business seminar.[10] Here is an overview of negotiating skills worth developing.

- Don't ask for something that is not possible, which makes you seem hostile or immature. The important thing is to establish your credibility instead.
- Be assertive. If you start high, it gives you room to move.
- Go slow in negotiating. If the conversation becomes too emotional, step back, breathe, change thought patterns, and ask questions.
- Always think creatively. Consider what is valuable to the employer and won't cost you too much to give. You have to understand the employer's goals and values to make a good assessment.
- Don't answer a probe. Probe back. If you can't respond reasonably—one way or the other—silence is always effective.
- Never say yes or no during a negotiation. Saying yes ends the negotiation too quickly, and saying no puts the other person on the defensive. Instead say, "Yes, if . . ."
- If you are giving away concessions, let your counterpart know. But don't pretend to be making concessions if you aren't. Stay honest . . . your credibility is at stake.
- Listen attentively, especially if the situation becomes emotionally intense.
- When the relationship and the outcome are equally important, you need to negotiate. If the relationship is more important than the outcome, then don't negotiate every last detail. (In other words, don't niggle yourself out of an offer.)
- When you make a concession, get a trade.
- Always make a good case for why you are negotiating.

A discussion of salary can push many individuals' emotional hot buttons, but, according to Bruzzese, women tend to be more vulnerable than men when the topic of money is put on the table. "I think women are probably weaker in terms of asking for what they want. Men have no problem with this generally. For them it's like bargaining for anything—like bargaining for a car. I think women are getting better, but I still think they get stuck in that feeling of, 'I should get this because I work hard and the employer should recognize that I work hard.' Well, guess what; sometimes it [hard work] goes unnoticed. And nobody will notice unless you call attention to it."

Sahadi also said that women tend to place more value on psychic income, such as: "internal pay equity, clear explanations of how performance is evaluated, effective supervisors . . . and a culture that recognizes the importance of a personal and family life."[11] Occasionally, however, women hold on longer than they should. Some women outgrow their positions, even though they know they can earn more money elsewhere, "because they like their bosses." Sahadi suggests that psychic income as well as better earnings are a real possibility at other companies, so avoid this "trap" and weigh all your options carefully.

Ruth Shlossman offered a different perspective: "I am not convinced that women are less effective negotiators. I think there are deeper sociological reasons why women make less than men in general. I personally think that most people are not effective in negotiating salaries. They don't know how to think out of the box and tend to negotiate for one thing only. We should all be negotiating such things as a career path, mentoring, future training, job assignments, a favorable review schedule, how we will be evaluated, and much more. We have to remember that we are negotiating our future career path when we negotiate our salary as well."

THE OFFER STAGE

Once the offer is made, you are in the best possible position to negotiate. You have determined the company is the perfect fit for your skills and qualifications, and the company believes you are the answer to its problem. The hiring manager often speaks to human resources, and together they come up with a figure that fits into their salary range. Verizon's Thonis said, "We work very closely with HR on [salary]. HR will come back and we'll know what we can offer. And we'll talk about a signing bonus or something like that. There are a number of things that we'll do."

Finally the moment you have been anticipating. The telephone rings. The HR representative tells you that the job is yours. Once you express your interest, the representative then gives you the details regarding the whole package. Take notes if you can. You may have heard it a thousand times, but everything *is* negotiable.

Listen carefully to every word. Then reaffirm your interest in the job to the company representative. Politely tell the person you will call him or her tomorrow—or whenever you finally feel comfortable enough to speak about the specifics without becoming emotional. Sleeping on the information is good, but don't linger too long.

Bruzzese said the appropriate time period for accepting an offer depends on the level of the position: "I always think it's a good idea to sleep on it—at least 24 hours—and the higher you go, the more time you can take, like three or four days. You don't want to stretch it beyond a week. But the higher you go, the more you have to think about, so it's always a good idea to sleep on it. I've learned . . . to get up and walk away. I'm a real 'Make your decision and go with your gut' person, but even I see the real value of taking a deep breath and giving it 24 hours . . . . Go call someone instead. You don't always have to do what that person says, but I think someone else's input is always valuable."

You may be totally smitten with the new job, so what do you need to consider?

First, you must be comfortable with the salary. Is it better than the one you were earning at your last job? Will the salary allow you to pay all your living expenses in the new locale? Is the salary below market, fair, or competitive? Your salary history is verifiable (even though not all employers check), so some employers may make an offer based on what you made at your last job (for instance, the employer knows for a fact that you earn $56,000 at your current job, so don't expect the offer to jump to $75,000). Employers are usually willing to offer 10 to 15 percent more than you made at your last job, so keep this in mind. Many experts agree that salary may be the least negotiable item in the whole package.

What if the salary is far below your expectations? Bruzzese said, "My feeling is that if a company is severely lowballing you, I always look for signs and indicators that you're not a good fit. And if the employer is playing lowball, [is the company] telling you that it's in financial trouble and . . . cannot pay the market rate? Maybe the HR person has absolutely no control over the budget or input in setting salaries. Those are little signs that the company is not operating as a team, and you may not be comfortable working in such an environment." You may even want to reconsider.

For many, salary is the bottom line when considering an offer. Because there may not be enough wiggle room in salary negotiation, the real bargaining may have to be reserved for the other items in the deal. For example, the new employer has strict policies regarding salary: All R&D associates with your experience and background make x amount of dollars, but they want you on board and are willing to lure you with a signing bonus. This is negotiable. The first thing you must do, though, is ask for it. Be reasonable and say, "I understand that you cannot offer me more salary because [blank], but I would like a signing bonus of [$blank] because I am worth it [blank, blank, blank]." If the employer pushes back, remember to stay away from definitive answers, such as yes (the negotiation is over) or no (defensiveness kicks in). Say instead, "Yes, if . . ." or "I will need another day to consider . . ."

Then ask more questions (as long as you haven't already asked these questions during the interview process). Maybe you can ask for more vacation time. Perhaps you neglected to ask when your salary will be reviewed again. Why not ask to have it reviewed in six months instead of a year? Maybe your partner has a comprehensive health care plan, and you want to opt out of the new company's plan. Can the employer make up the difference somewhere else? What about stock options? Or a flexible schedule? Feel free to bargain and trade, but don't niggle yourself out of a job either. Listen for the cue *enough is enough*. So much depends on the manner in which you pursue these discussions. Always remain polite, reasonable, and calm during the negotiation process. In an article in *Fortune*, Dick Parsons, chairman and CEO of Time Warner, advises: "When you negotiate, leave a little something on the table."[12]

BCI's Horton said candidates usually get "one shot to see if the employer is flexible. You definitely should [come back and] try one time [to boost the salary]. If that doesn't work, then you ask for a week's more vacation, a better benefits package. Or you can negotiate who you are going to report to. Or what exactly your role is going to be. When are you up for your next review? Instead of six months, ask for a three-month review."

Ultimately, it always comes down to how much you want the new job.

Engelhard's Mangiarano said he knows what the candidate expects to earn at his company at the time of the offer. If the candidate makes a compelling case that he or she is the perfect fit for the job and then ups the ante, Mangiarano has to make a decision: "Is the individual so special that I'm willing to pay more than I normally would to have him or her join our company? That's my decision to make."

Fit also plays a part at small companies. According to BCI's Horton, "I want the right fit. And usually $10,000 or $15,000 is not going to make or break the bank to get the right candidate." It rests on you to convince the employer that you are worth every penny that you are asking for.

IRONING OUT THE DETAILS

A lot of facts and figures have been bandied about during this process. If you didn't take notes during the interview, then sit down as soon as possible to gather your thoughts. If the offer is accepted, many companies wrap up all the details of a negotiation with an employment contract. Always read the fine print. If an employment contract is not offered to you, make sure you write down the details of *all* of your conversations with hiring managers as well as the individuals in human resources with whom you spoke.

Bruzzese said, "It depends on the job you're going for. I think you should definitely get in writing your start date, your salary, the benefits you're going to be offered, your job description, who you are reporting to, when your performance evaluations will be because sometimes it's an honest mistake, where human resources and the people hiring you don't exactly communicate it down to the manager level, to the actual supervisor you'll be working with."

So take the initiative and put it in writing. If the company doesn't offer you a contract, then put the details of the negotiation in a letter that confirms your acceptance of the job. You should then mail this letter to the representative in human resources who was your primary contact. Going on record is a testament to your professionalism. (Just make sure to keep a copy for yourself as well.) This way there will be no miscommunication. Everyone is on the same page and you can proceed comfortably. If the company doesn't offer you an employment contract, Figure 10.1 shows a sample letter you should send once you accept the offer.

The point is that so much information is exchanged during the interview process that it is not uncommon for misunderstandings to arise. Better to start out, as Bruzzese referred to it, "on the same page," then to have to backtrack later. It is always better to express yourself clearly from the get-go. Put it in writing and never be shy about the terms of an agreement. You worked hard for them.

CONGRATULATIONS!

Everything—in business and in life—revolves around solid, working relationships. People (and companies) are imperfect, and there are times when you have to sweat some bullets to iron out misunderstandings; but keep in mind what Ross Perot once said: "Business is not just doing deals; business is having great products, doing great engineering, and providing tremendous service to customers. Finally, business is a cobweb of human relationships." Build a path of advancement that takes everyone into consideration as you move forward.

And congratulations! All your hard work has paid off handsomely, and now you have a new job that will challenge you and catapult you to new heights. Don't forget to thank every person you spoke to during the interview process for their time. In fact, even if you decline the offer, it is still a good idea to recognize these people. Remember, this is your industry—not as big and anonymous as you think—and your reputation is only as good as you make it. Observe protocol and then go the extra mile. People appreciate your gratitude, and you'll be able to sleep soundly as a result.

As the Fortune 500 hiring professionals said again and again, "Be yourself!" Say what you mean in plain English, work hard, and treat others well.

Finally, good luck!

FIGURE 10.1 *Sample Acceptance Letter*

Mr. John Smith
1 Oak Drive
Oakridge, IL 60600

June 30, 2006

Ms. Mary Smith
XYZ Company
1 Maple Avenue
Oakridge, IL 60601

Dear Ms. Smith:

Thank you for the offer to work at XYZ Company. I am eager to begin on July 1, 2005.

I appreciate all the time you spent talking with me, and I would like to reaffirm some of the details of our conversation. I understand that I will be working for Alice Smith, the manager, in the finance department as a Level II accountant, and I will be making a salary of $48,000. Although your comprehensive benefits package is appealing, I'm glad we were able to agree that I will opt out of the package and instead increase my vacation to six weeks instead of the standard three. Also agreed upon is my performance evaluation, which will take place in December 2006 instead of June 2007. I admire your flexibility during our discussion.

Please contact me if you have any questions regarding this information. I can be reached at (000) 000-0000 (cell). Again, thank you and I look forward to working at XYZ.

Sincerely,

John Smith

Preface

1. Matt Peiken, *Pioneer Press,* "56 Cellists: 1 Position," September 21, 2004:1.

Acknowledgments

1. *Fortune,* April 5, 2004: F-1–F-20.

Chapter 1

1. Milt Freudenheim, "More Help Wanted: Older Workers Please Apply," *New York Times,* March 23, 2005: A1+.

2. David Koeppel, "What to Do When the Ideal Job Proves Not to Be as Advertised," *New York Times,* March 27, 2005: Section 10, 1+.

3. All percentages are based on the number of respondents who answered a particular question.

4. Cal Fussman, "Jeff Bezos, Founder and CEO of Amazon.com," *Esquire,* January 2002.

Chapter 2

1. Richard Bolles, *What Color Is Your Parachute? A Practical Manual for Job-Hunters and Career-Changers* (Berkeley: Ten Speed Press, 2004): 243.

2. Matthew Kelly, *The Rhythm of Life: Living Every Day with Passion and Purpose* (New York: Fireside Publishers, 2004): 5–7.

3. Brenda Greene, *Get the Interview Every Time* (Chicago: Dearborn Trade, 2004).

4. Rutgers University, http://www.careerservices.rutgers.edu/career. In addition to research on Rutgers' Career Services Web site, an interview was con-

ducted with Crystal McArthur, the associate director of Career Services at Rutgers University, on January 31, 2005.

5. University of South Carolina, http://www.sc.edu/career.

6. Ohio State University, http://www.osu.edu/student/acedrs/career.

7. University of Nebraska (Lincoln), http://www.unl.edu/careers.

8. University of California (Santa Cruz), http://www2.ucsc.edu/careers/.

9. University of Oregon, http://lcb.uoregon.edu/career.

10. Jannell Kingsborough, "New course preps students for careers," *The BG News*, November 17, 2004.

11. University of New Mexico, Career Builder Series Workshops, http://www.career.unm.edu/grad/workshops.php.

12. Massachusetts Division of Career Services, http://www.detma.org.

13. New York State Department of Labor, Workforce New York "Career Zone," http://www.labor.state.ny.us/.

14. Occupational Information Network, O*Net OnLine, http://online.onetcenter.org/.

15. Bolles, *What Color Is Your Parachute?*, Chapter 8 (Note 1 above).

16. Occupational Information Network.

17. Katharine Hansen, "Strategic Portrayal of Transferable Job Skills Is a Vital Job-Search Technique," http://www.quintcareers.com.

18. The Princeton Review, free Career Quiz, http://www.princetonreview.com/cte/quiz/career_quiz1.asp.

19. Quintessential Careers. "Online Career Assessment Tools Review," http://www.quintcareers.com/online_assessment_review.html.

20. Anita Bruzzese, "Keep Track of Your Value to the Company," *Salt Lake Tribune*, January 23, 2005. http://www.sltrib.com/business/ci_2533638.

21. Lominger, the Leadership Architects. Lominger Career Architect®, http://www.lominger.com/67_336.htm.

22. University of Ottawa, *Core Competency Development Guide*. For the language to describe the work you do, review this guide. Access the guide at http://www.uottawa.ca/services/hr/perf/Devcoeng.pdf.

23. Morgan Stanley, job posting, February 7, 2005, http://www.morganstanley.com/careers/index.html.

24. Alltel, http://www.alltel.com/career/index.html.

25. Nick Corcodillos. "Ten Stupid Hiring Mistakes," November 10, 2004, www.asktheheadhunter.com/hatenmistakes1.htm.

26. Comcast, 2003 annual report, http://www.comcast.com.

27. IRIN, Annual Report Resource Center, http://www.irin.com.

28. Hoover's Online, http://www.hoovers.com.

29. Michael Laskoff, "How to Handle Informational Interviews," *Business-Week,* September 3, 2003. http://www.businessweek.com/careers/contents/sep2003/ca2003093_4973_ca2009.htm.

30. *Campus Recruiting and Job Search Manual* (Purdue University: Career Recruitment Media, Inc., 1999–2004). http://purdue.placementmanual.com.

Chapter 3

1. Edmund L. Andrews and Eduardo Porter, "As Businesses Step Up Spending, Some See a Just-Right Economy," *New York Times,* March 7, 2005: Section C, 1+.

2. Alan Horowitz, "How to Ace the Telephone Interview," *ComputerWorld,* June 2, 2003. http://www.computerworld.com/careertopics/careers/story/0,10801,8167,00.html.

3. Robert Half Technology Associates, "Phone Screening," http://www.roberthalftechnology.com/RHT/PhoneScreening.

4. Penn State Career Services, "The Site Interview: What to Expect," http://www.sa.psu.edu/career/pdf/CG_interview.pdf.

5. National Association of Colleges and Employers, "Communication Skills, Honesty/Integrity Top Employers' 'Wish List' for Job Candidates," January 20, 2005, www.naceweb.org/press/display.asp?year=&prid=207.

6. Rod and Eversley Farnbach, *Overcoming Performance Anxiety* (Australia: Simon and Schuster, 2001): 6.

7. Bureau of Labor Statistics, http://www.bls.gov. For more information, take a look at *Working in the 21st Century.* Single copies of the printed version of *Working in the 21st Century* are available. To obtain a copy, send an e-mail to blsdata_staff@bls.gov with your mailing address included in your request; or mail a request to the Office of Publications and Special Studies, U.S. Department of Labor, Bureau of Labor Statistics, Washington DC 20212; or call 202-691-5200.

8. Lisa Belkin, "Take This Job and Hug It," *New York Times,* February 13, 2005: Section 10, 1.

9. Bob Rosner, "Working Wounded: Interview with Confidence," October 24, 2004. http://www.jobjournal.com/article_full_text.asp?artid=1281.

Chapter 4

1. Amy Larocca, "Yoko, Now," *New York,* February 14, 2004. http://newyork-metro.com/nymetro/shopping/fashion/spring05/11012.

2. Jeremy W. Peters, "Company's Smoking Ban Means Off-Hours Too," *New York Times,* February 8, 2005: Section C, 5.

3. Liz Ryan, "Getting the Most from Your References," *BusinessWeek,* June 16, 2004. http://www.businessweek.com/careers/content/jun2004/ca20040616_7777_ca009.htm.

4. PSEG. The company's reference report comes from this site: http://skill survey.com/HCM_main.php.

5. Connie Thompson, "Credit Checks on Job Applications?" August 28, 2001, http://www.komotv.com/news/story.asp?ID=13618.

6. For more information about background checks, go to the Privacy Rights Clearinghouse and review *Employment Background Checks: A Jobseeker's Guide* at http://www.privacyrights.org/fs/fs16-bck.htm. Another article to review is "Background Checks Gaining," by Janna Braun in the *Arizona Business Gazette.* It can be accessed at http://azcentral.com/abgnews/article/0812background12.html. And for a lighter take on the subject, see Liz Pulliam Weston's article, "Secrets a Background Check Won't Uncover," at http://moneycentral.msn.com/content/Banking/FinancialPrivacy/P41877./asp. For a free background check on yourself, see http://www.backgroundcheckgateway.com. This company posts a privacy clause stating that they will not sell this information to anyone.

7. David Koeppel, "What to Do When the Ideal Job Proves Not to Be as Advertised," *New York Times,* March 27, 2005: Section 10, 1.

Chapter 5

1. Jeffrey Fox, *How to Become a Great Boss* (New York: Hyperion, 2002): 21.

2. Greene, *Get the Interview Every Time* (Chapter 2, note 3).

3. Rosner, "Interview with Confidence" (Chapter 3, note 9).

4. Allan Schweyer, "Case Study: Wynn Casino Las Vegas," Human Capital Institute, http://www.humancapitalinstitute.org/hci/hci.home.

5. Kelly, *The Rhythm of Life* (Chapter 2, note 2).

6. William Zinsser, *On Writing Well* (New York: HarperPerennial, 1998): 6.

7. James Waldroop and Timothy Butler, *Maximum Success* (New York: Currency/Doubleday, 2000). The entire book is highly recommended reading.

8. Anne Fisher, "Starting a New Job, Don't Blow It," *Fortune,* March 7, 2005: 48.

9. *Insurance Journal.* "Happy with Your Boss? New Survey Reports Contempt for Managers Across the Board," January 21, 2005.

10. Lominger, the Leadership Architects. Lominger Career Architect® http://www.lominger.com/67_336.htm.

11. George Favre, "The Art of Interviewing," The Poynter Institute, October 22, 2001, http://poynter.org/content_view.asp?id=5165.

Chapter 6

1. PSEG, Careers, http://www.pseg.com.

2. BellSouth, Careers, http://www.bellsouth.com.

3. Jason Olson, "From the Soup to the Nuts. A Blog: Microsoft Interview," http://geekswithblogs.net/jolson/archive/2005/01/21/20636.aspx.

4. John Mongan and Noah Suojanen, *Programming Interviews Exposed* (New York: John Wiley & Sons, 2000).

5. William Poundstone, *How Would You Move Mount Fuji? Microsoft's Cult of the Puzzle–How the World's Smartest Companies Select the Most Creative Thinkers* (New York: Little, Brown, 2003).

6. ACES (American Copy Editors Society), "Editing Booklet," http://www.copydesk.org/guidelines.htm.

7. Bill Walsh, "How Can I Become a Copy Editor?" http://www.theslot.com/howto.html.

8. Greene, *Get the Interview Every Time* (Chapter 2, note 3).

Chapter 7

1. Jim Collins, *Good to Great.* (New York: HarperBusiness, 2001).

2. Bolles, *What Color Is Your Parachute?* (Chapter 2, note 1).

3. Anita Bruzzese, "Employee Satisfaction Slacks Off After Time." *Detroit News,* March 7, 2005. http://www.detnews.com/2005/money/0503/07/B01-10932.htm.

4. Waldroop and Butler, *Maximum Success* (Chapter 5, note 7).

Chapter 9

1. Dennis Overbye, "A Philanthropist of Science Seeks to Be Its Next Nobel," *New York Times,* April 19, 2005: Section F, 1+.

2. "How to Handle Illegal Interview Questions," E-zine. CollegeGrad.com. http://www.collegegrad.com/ezine/23illega.shtml. CollegeGrad.com is a very useful site for newcomers to the job market.

3. Ronald Krannich, "38 Illegal, Sensitive, and Stupid Interview Questions . . . and How to Respond," *Washington Post,* April 11, 2004. Courtesy of Impact Publications.

4. Catholic University, "Interview Guidelines," http://humanresources.cua.edu/manager/guidelines.cfm.

5. Nicholas Confessore, "Older Hands Find Place in a New Course," *New York Times,* February 20, 2005: Section 10, 1.

6. Eilene Zimmerman, "Doing Well in Your Career by Doing Good Outside It," *New York Times,* February 27, 2005.

7. Bolles, *What Color Is Your Parachute?* (Chapter 2, note 1).

8. Anne Fisher, "How to Battle the Coming Brain Drain," *Fortune,* March 21, 2005.

9. Milt Freudenheim, "More Help Wanted," *New York Times,* March 23, 2005 (Chapter 1, note 1).

10. Anne Fisher, "Ask Annie" column, *Fortune,* December 13, 2004.

Chapter 10

1. Waldroop and Butler, *Maximum Success* (Chapter 5, note 7).

2. University of South Carolina, Career Center, "Successful Salary Negotiations." http://www.sc.edu/career.

3. Skidmore College, Career Services, "Evaluating Job Offers and Negotiating Salary." http://www.skidmore.edu/administration/career/handoutsWeb/index.html.

4. Nick Cocodilos, Ask the Headhunter, "Divulging salary history," http://www.asktheheadhunter.com/faqsalary1.htm.

5. 1st-Writer.com, "Salary History and Salary Requirements," http://www.1st-writer.com/Salary.htm.

6. Jeanne Sahadi, "Feeling Underpaid? Try This," July 18, 2003. http://money.cnn.com/2003/07/17/commentary/everyday/sahadi.

7. Bureau of Labor Statistics, http://www.bls.com.

8. WSJ.com, http://www.collegejournal.com/salarydata.

9. Greene, *Get the Interview Every Time* (Chapter 2, note 3).

10. Watershed Associates, Ruth Shlossman, Negotiation Seminar. www.watershedassociates.com.

11. Sahadi, "Feeling Underpaid? Try This" (Note 6).

12. "The Best Advice I Ever Got," *Fortune,* March 21, 2005.

13. Interviews were conducted with Ted Horton of BCI Partners and Anita Bruzzesse, a Gannett career columnist and author of *Take This Job and Thrive,* in March 2005. Ruth Shlossman's negotiating seminar for Watershed Associates forms the basis of the negotiating skills section of this chapter. Additional questions were answered by Shlossman via e-mail in April 2005.

Ace Your Interview: The Wetfeet Insider Guide to Interviewing. San Francisco: Wetfeet, 2004.

Bolles, Richard. *What Color Is Your Parachute?* Berkeley: Ten Speed Press, 2004.

Bruzzese, Anita. *Take this Job and Thrive.* Manassas Park, Virginia: Impact Publications, 2000.

Collins, Jim. *Good to Great.* New York: HarperBusiness, 2001.

Cunningham, Helen, and Brenda Greene. *The Business Style Handbook: An A-to-Z Guide for Writing on the Job with Tips from Communication Experts at the Fortune 500.* New York: McGraw-Hill, 2002.

DeLuca, Matthew. *Best Answers to the 201 Most Frequently Asked Interview Questions.* New York: McGraw-Hill, 1997.

Fox, Jeffrey. *How to Become a Great Boss.* New York: Hyperion, 2002.

Greene, Brenda. *Get the Interview Every Time: Fortune 500 Hiring Professionals' Tips for Writing Winning Resumes and Cover Letters.* Chicago: Dearborn Trade, 2004.

Kador, John. *201 Best Questions to Ask on Your Interview.* New York: McGraw-Hill, 2002.

Richardson, Bradley G. *Jobsmarts for Twentysomethings.* New York: Vintage Books, 1995.

Waldroop, James, and Timothy Butler. *Maximum Success: Changing the 12 Behavior Patterns that Keep You from Getting Ahead.* New York: Currency/Doubleday, 2000.

Zinsser, William. *On Writing Well.* New York: Harper Perennial, 1998.